Life Injections II

Further Connections Of Scripture To The Human Experience

Richard E. Zajac

CSS Publishing Company, Inc., Lima, Ohio

LIFE INJECTIONS II

For more information about CSS Publishing Company resources, visit our website at
www.csspub.com.

ISBN 0-7880-1875-2   PRINTED IN U.S.A.

In loving memory of my niece,
Julie Anna Zajac,
who helped make this book possible.

"She competed well!
She finished the race!
She kept the faith!"

Table Of Contents

Foreword

On November 18, 1965, the fathers of the Second Vatican Council promulgated the Dogmatic Constitution on Divine Revelation, Dei Verbum. In the prologue of this second document, the Council fathers emphasize the importance of God's Word in the lives of the faithful. "Hearing the Word of God reverently and proclaiming it confidently, this Holy Synod ... wants the whole world to hear the summons to salvation, so that through hearing, it may believe, through belief, it may hope, through hope, it may come to love."

From my experience of more than fifty years in the priesthood, the Constitution, Dei Verbum, has done wonders in transforming many of the clergy from a cultic to a servant model of ministry. In the first 25 years of my experience in parish ministry, preaching the Word of God did not seem to hold a high priority. Preaching at Sunday Mass was often suspended during warm weather. To be specific, a moratorium on the preached Word often took place from Memorial Day, the end of May, to Labor Day, early September. Very seldom was there a sermon at a funeral or a wedding. Preaching at weekday Mass was just never done. The structure of the Mass was divided into the Mass of the Catechumens and the Mass of the Faithful. The former, which contained a Word Service, was never considered an essential part of the celebration. Note the catechism reply to the query: "What are the three principal parts of the Mass?" The correct answer: "The Offertory, the Consecration, and the Communion." In addition, the average Catholic for the most part was ignorant when it came to knowledge of Sacred Scripture. To ask a devout parishioner about an interpretation of First Thessalonians, he or she may inquire as to whether it was a breakfast cereal.

At the outset of the Second Vatican Council, Blessed John XXIII is said to have remarked to a group of Council Fathers: "The Counter-Reformation is over. Now, my Council begins." Catholic reaction to some of the Reformers' insistence on the unique role of the Bible in the matter of salvation has come to an end. Sacred

7

Scripture has experienced a rebirth in Catholicism. We are happy to note that some of the best Biblicists in the world today are Catholic scholars. The Mass is divided now into the Liturgy of the Word and the Liturgy of the Eucharist. Homilies are preached, not only at every weekend celebration, but often at daily Mass. Beautiful words founded on Scripture are now proclaimed at weddings, funerals, and, in fact, at every Liturgy celebrated in the Church.

The author of *Life Injections II*, the Reverend Richard E. Zajac, is, in my view, a wonderful symbol of this rebirth of the Word. Richard Zajac came to be my associate in ministry when I was called to be the pastor of St. Ambrose Parish, a large urban community in South Buffalo, New York. "Duke" Zajac, and that's how he's called by all his friends, came to us fresh from the oils of his ordination to the priesthood. It was June of 1976. From the outset, I could not help but notice how laboriously he worked to prepare a Sunday homily. He would literally spend hours at this work. Going to celebrate Mass at an early hour on Saturday morning, I would pass by Duke's room. He had been at his desk from the break of dawn hoping to make God's Word take root in the lives of our people. This is the second volume of *Life Injections*. Like the first volume, these words have been shared with the congregations when Father Zajac celebrated Word and Eucharist.

Msgr. William G. Stanton
Pastor Emeritus
St. Ambrose Church
Buffalo, New York
2001

Introduction

Thanks to the success of my first publication and thanks to the support and encouragement of many friends, I present to you my second volume of reflections on the Sunday Scriptures. They are a cleaned and polished version of what was preached from the pulpit of Sisters Hospital over the past several years. Their path from my head to the written page has been a long and arduous one.

They all began with a yellow pad and a Lectionary and the hope beyond hope that an idea for a sermon will spring to mind the minute the Scriptures for the given Sunday are read. Unfortunately, that rarely occurs. Then, having read countless numbers of sermons from such preaching giants as Harry Emerson Fosdick, Halford Luccock, J. Wallace Hamilton, and F.W. Boreham and having listened to the tapes of hundreds of sermons from the likes of Bruce W. Thielemann and R. Maurice Boyd and John Gladstone, my next hope is that I've penciled into the margin of the Lectionary a reference to one that touched upon the given Sunday's readings. I say a prayer that a review of that sermon will provide for an idea with which I might run. Unfortunately that, too, rarely occurs. I'm then left with searching through the homiletic aids to which I subscribe usually only to find that they have little to offer, leaving me to wonder why I had wasted good money on their subscription. In the end, I'm left with my head spinning as to what I'll preach about. So I'll step away from the process and go about my hospital duties and inevitably an idea will be born. That's when the real work begins.

I keep on my desk a gray file of index cards alphabetized according to themes. Whenever I come across a twist or angle on one of those themes from a book I may have read, I note that on the appropriate index card. Since I've kept the file a long time, I may have upwards of 40 notations on a single theme. So should I, for example, decide to preach on an idea relating to, let's say, risk or joy or suffering, I'll check the index card so labeled and I'll go through the various books listed and read the pages I had noted. If from that reading something stands out as an interesting point relative to the idea being pursued, I'll jot it down on a small yellow pad. Once this bit of research is complete, I then move to the story file.

That file is kept in a black box that sits on wheels not far from my desk. It contains anecdotes, stories, fables, analogies, statistics, or jokes, all of which have been xeroxed from books I've read through the years. Since I read on the average of forty books a year, it amounts to a fairly large file, a foot and a half high, to be exact. Having the idea I wish to preach about in my mind along with the points jotted down on that small yellow pad, I then go through every single entry in that file, throwing aside whichever one might, even remotely, illustrate that idea or that point. That's close to a six-hour process.

Once completed, I take the "tossed aside" stories, anecdotes, etc., and give them a second look and a second review, discarding some while sorting the others. The sorting process could leave as many as eight or nine piles of papers scattered around my chair, each representing a particular thought relative to the idea on which I will preach. Those piles become the clay I use to mold the sermon.

So with yellow pad in hand and the sorted images around my chair, I begin the most difficult phase of all, which is the actual writing of the sermon. The opening image holds the key, for it will set the tone for what follows; so the selecting of one is the most delicate piece of the writing process. Once selected, I can proceed, often only to find that I've written myself into a corner. That will necessitate staring at a blank page for what seems like hours hoping for a way out. In the end, I'll have filled seven yellow pages with my hen-scratching, complete with innumerable cross-outs and arrows and that will represent the first draft of my sermon.

The next phase is more tedious than painstaking. It involves the copying of the draft onto white copy paper using a combination of writing and printing. For some lines I'll use large strokes and others small; it's done that way so I might easily reference the text when I preach. It's the text I'll ultimately take to the pulpit.

Once I've completed the transfer from the yellow sheets onto the white, I'll place it aside. Then a day or two before I am to preach, I'll take the text and edit it with a black magic marker, changing words and sentences here and there, hoping and praying that there won't be any need for major surgery. Once this final phase is complete, there's still the need for reading it several times over and practicing it so as to assure a smooth and vibrant delivery. From start to finish, you're looking at 24 hours of work.

The sermons you are about to read have been the ones I've felt were well received and fairly effective. They represent a span of six years. They also represent the work of my niece Julie Zajac as well as Barbara Mroz of Expressly for Women, an arm of Sisters Hospital. They were gracious and generous enough to type them into a computer, saving me from that burdensome task. I hope you'll enjoy reading the following sermons. I hope they'll speak to your life.

It Doesn't Pay

Scripture Lesson: Matthew 18:21-35
"... I say seven times seventy times ..."

Withholding forgiveness can be detrimental to our character and well-being.

A forest ranger at Yellowstone National Park led a group of tourists to an area of the forest where they could safely observe the activity of a grizzly bear. Lights were situated in such a way that they could see the bear but the bear couldn't see them and, at the moment, the bear was feasting on some food that had been purposely placed opposite those lights. The ranger then began to lecture the tourists on the behavior and activity of the grizzly, citing the bear as the strongest and most powerful creature in the Park and explaining how he would often tear to shreds any animal that crossed his path, especially while he was eating.

Just then, a skunk emerged from the woods and began to help himself to the bear's food. The grizzly made no attempt to stop him. The tourists asked the ranger why it was and how it was that the grizzly didn't tear the skunk to shreds. The ranger paused and said: "The grizzly learned long ago that it doesn't pay."

I begin with that anecdote because I'd like to talk with you today as to why it doesn't pay to withhold forgiveness, why it doesn't pay to nurse grudges, to wallow in bitterness, to maintain resentment, or to loathe one's enemies. When Jesus told Peter in the Gospel that he should forgive seven times seventy times, he was trying to keep Peter from being sprayed by a skunk; he was trying to keep Peter from suffering the consequences that arise from the withholding of forgiveness.

Rabbi Harold Kushner, in his latest book,[1] talks of counseling a wife and mother whose husband left her for another woman several years earlier. He's now fallen behind in his child support payments and that's only added fuel to her mounting resentment and bitterness. When the rabbi suggested that she forgive her husband, her response was: "How do you expect me to forgive him after what he's done to me and my children?" The rabbi's response was classic! He said: "I'm not asking you to forgive him because what he did wasn't terrible, it was terrible! I'm suggesting that you forgive him because he doesn't deserve to have the power to turn you into a bitter and resentful woman!"

Think of it! When we hate an ex-spouse, when we hate a former friend, when we hate anyone, we're giving them power over our sleep, power over our nerves, and power over our peace of mind. Our enemies would dance for joy if they knew how our hatred was hurting us while not hurting them in the least.

So when Jesus told Peter to forgive seven times seventy times, he was trying to keep Peter from succumbing to the power of his enemies. And, at the same time, he was also trying to keep him from ill health.

I remember reading the case of a doctor who had a patient suddenly arrive in his office with crippling rheumatoid arthritis. The disease had been under control for some time but it was obvious that something had exacerbated her condition for her hands were now doubled up like claws. A thorough examination revealed no physical reason for the change so he asked: "Has anything unusual happened to you recently?" "Oh, yes!" she replied. "I know exactly what you mean and furthermore I have no intention of forgiving him!" The doctor couldn't find out who she was talking about or what had happened, but apparently at that point in her life nursing resentment was more important to her than her health.

It's been documented in many a medical journal as to the ill effects that arise when forgiveness is withheld, how when people decide to stew and wallow in bitterness and anger their blood pressure is negatively affected as is the lining of their stomach and their entire cardiovascular system. The withholding of forgiveness can shorten one's life considerably.

I read of a recent study which revealed that one out of every five victims of a fatal car accident had a quarrel within six hours before his or her accident. So if we're fighting with an enemy or even a friend, if we walk way from a dispute without practicing forgiveness, it may not only harm our physical health but it may so affect our mental health and alertness that we could be open prey for a serious, if not fatal, accident.

So when Jesus told Peter to forgive seven times seventy times, he was trying to keep Peter from succumbing to the power of his enemies, he was trying to keep Peter from ill health, and he was also trying to keep Peter from making a tragic mistake.

A woman's answering machine recorded a message from a teacher asking her to call about her son's irresponsible behavior. The teacher left no number so the woman couldn't let her know that she misdialed the call. A day later, another misdialed call informed Bob of a schedule change for an important business meeting. Again, no number was left. The woman wondered what impact these two mistakes would have on the people involved. Would the teacher wrongly judge that the mother didn't care enough to return the call? Would Bob's boss wrongly judge his missing that meeting as an act of irresponsibility?

Wrong judgments, as you can see, are easy to make. So it could well be that what we're mad about when it comes to someone else, what may have fueled a grudge we happen to be holding, may have no basis whatsoever in truth or fact. It could well be that we misinterpreted or wrongly judged a particular action or lack of action and all our anger, resentment, and hate has been directed toward someone who didn't deserve that anger or resentment or hate.

And how about the reality of our making mountains out of molehills, our raising to a high level someone or something of little importance or concern? Forgiveness can spare us that!

There's a story about a speaker who was giving a lecture after which she passed out sheets of paper for the audience to write down their name along with a question that she might answer and discuss. Once collected, she began to answer them one at a time. When she came to the sixth sheet of paper, on it was the word "idiot" written in bold letters. She read the one letter word out loud and then looked at the audience. "Ladies and gentlemen!" she announced. "Over the years, I have frequently received replies where the sender has written the question and forgotten to sign his name. This, however, is the first time the writer has signed his name and forgotten to write the question!"

How often has it happened where we've gotten angry and resentful and bitter over someone or something of "idiot" quality, someone or something that we shouldn't have allowed to get under our skin? Far too many times, instead of forgiving a comment from a foolish source, instead of forgiving an incident that spoke to childishness and immaturity and vulgarity, we raise it to a standard it didn't deserve. We make the molehill a mountain. We invest a tremendous amount of negative emotion in someone or something we should have treated as unworthy of our attention.

So when Jesus told Peter to forgive seven times seventy times, he was trying to keep Peter from succumbing to the power of his enemies; he was trying to keep Peter from ill health; he was trying to keep Peter from a tragic mistake; he was trying to keep Peter from raising to a high level someone or something of little importance; and he was trying to keep Peter from tarnishing his character.

Elie Wiesel in the book titled *Night*[2] (his story of the Holocaust) writes that, after their liberation from the Nazi concentration camps, he and others put revenge out of their minds. They did so, first because they survived and that was more important than revenge. And most especially and most importantly, they did so because they realized that revenge would have meant their descending to the level of those who put them through their horror.

The great Booker T. Washington, who endured much racial prejudice, once said: "I will permit no person to narrow and degrade my soul by making me hate him!"

All too often when we withhold forgiveness, all too often when we decide to nurse bitterness and hatred and resentment, we're portraying qualities that do not speak well of us. We're portraying qualities very similar to the ones we despised in the person who's the target of our bitterness and hatred and resentment.

I believe it was Saint Augustine who said: "Imagine the vanity of thinking that your enemy can do you more damage than your enmity!"

Lastly, I believe Jesus told Peter to forgive seven times seventy times to keep him from the embarrassment of acknowledging his own imperfection.

I like the story of Sid and Barney out for a round of golf. To make the game more interesting, they made a five-dollar bet as to who would have the lowest score. After the seventeenth hole, Barney is ahead by a stroke but slices his ball into the rough on the eighteenth. "Help me find my ball!" he says to Sid and the two of them head for the rough to look for the lost ball. After five minutes, neither has any luck. Since a lost ball carries a one-stroke penalty, Barney secretly throws another ball into the rough and yells to his partner that he found his lost ball. Sid looks at him and shakes his head in disgust. "After all these years we've been friends, do you mean to tell me that you'd cheat me on golf for a measly five bucks?" "What do you mean, cheat?" asks Barney. "I found my ball sitting right here!" "And you're a liar, too!" says Sid in amazement. "I'll have you know I've been standing on your ball for the last five minutes!"

One of the problems with holding back on forgiveness is that quite often there's an air of self-righteousness around it. There's this idea that we're pure and pristine, that we're devoid of any faults, that we've never done anything in our lives for which we might need forgiveness. Like Sid, we'll get mad and resentful at Barney when, in fact, Barney had every reason to be mad and resentful at us. Being forgiving can save us the embarrassment of admitting that we have faults and shortcomings just like everyone else.

That grizzly bear at the Park did not swing his paw and tear apart that skunk because he knew it didn't pay. It would behoove us to listen to Jesus on forgiving seven times seventy times because, in fact, to withhold forgiveness doesn't pay.

It gives our enemy the undeserved power to turn us into a bitter and resentful person. It can flare up our rheumatoid arthritis, our ulcers, and our blood pressure. It can have us hating someone who didn't do what he or she was judged to have done. It can have us getting hot and bothered over someone or something that didn't deserve our attention. It can lower us to the level of our enemy. It can have us angry with a golf partner while, at the same time, admitting that we're standing on the lost ball.

My friends, heed the words of Jesus! Forgive seven times seventy times!

---

1. Harold S. Kushner, *How Good Do We Have To Be* (New York: Little, Brown & Company, 1996).

2. Elie Wiesel, *Night* (New York: Hill & Wang, 1960).

Juxtaposing

Scripture Lesson: John 3:14-21
"... God so loved the world ..."

Some down-to-earth applications of what my father would have
called a "fifty-cent word."

Tom Toles, the political cartoonist for *The Buffalo News*, has
drawn many interesting and provocative cartoons throughout the
years. What, for me, ranks as his all-time best was one drawn around
Christmas a decade or so ago. He drew a picture of a little girl on
Santa Claus' lap with a list spilling down to the floor. She had this
huge smile as she was going over the list with Santa. Out of her
mouth were printed the words: "Barbie doll, stereo, and Apple computer." Right next to the little girl at the bottom right corner of the
cartoon was a picture of a black Ethiopian child with a distended
belly. He's standing next in line to see Santa and he's carrying an
empty bowl and Toles has him picking up on the end of the little
girl's conversation for he's mouthing the word "Apple" with a look
of longing and desperation. No one preached a more powerful sermon that Christmas.

I reference that Tom Toles creation because of the technique
he used to make his point. He set one picture up against another; he
juxtaposed two images and in so doing he drew a powerful contrast between our children and those of the Third World. He employed the technique of juxtaposing, a technique often used by political cartoonists as well as artists to give some perspective to an
issue, a cause, or a problem in need of our attention.

Juxtaposing is not something reserved for art professionals;
it's something with which we're all familiar. We juxtapose quite
readily and quite freely. The problem we have is that, in all too
many cases, we don't juxtapose correctly. We don't put the proper
picture next to the picture of our experience. We fail to image a
suitable companion to the object of our vision. There's no great

reminder of what needs to be seen and considered in light of what we're viewing or experiencing. When, by chance, we do happen to juxtapose correctly, when the right picture and image does come into our line of sight, there's no telling as to its positive effect.

I was recently on a panel with two other priests. Our purpose for gathering was to help Catholics who were mad at the Church, who had left the faith because of some experience in their past. What proved to be a constant was the fact that they juxtaposed incorrectly. They matched their one negative experience with a priest or a nun with the image of the Church. There were some who had a priest yell at them, some who had a priest or nun abuse them, and some, with tears in their eyes, recounted a horrible exchange of words between themselves and their priest. In a good majority of the cases, they then juxtaposed the image of that priest or nun with everyone who wore a Roman collar or a habit and then extended that image to the Church, failing to realize that the Church is much bigger than one priest or one nun.

That kind of juxtaposing is not something unique to disgruntled Catholics, but it's something which I'm afraid all of us have done on one occasion or another in our own life. It may not have been a priest we had a problem with, but it may have been somebody with black skin or someone who was of Irish, or Italian, or Polish, or German, or Jewish descent, or someone of a different sexual orientation. Because of what may have happened between us and them, because we may have observed some negative behavior in one of their representatives, we automatically juxtapose that image to everyone with black skin, or everyone who is Italian, or Polish, or gay, or lesbian. Juxtaposing in such a fashion has hardened many hearts and has fed the problem of prejudice.

I like that story of the mother who is very worried about her daughter's first day at school which was also the first day of integration in a formerly all-white setting. Running to meet the bus at the conclusion of the school day, she cautiously asked her daughter how it went. The daughter said she spent the day sitting next to a very friendly girl. The mother then asked the question she was afraid to ask: "Was she black?" "Yes," said her daughter. "What happened?" asked the mom. "Oh, nothing, we were both so scared we held hands all day."

The beauty of children is that they juxtapose correctly. They see people in much broader ways than we do. They don't connect them to one image or one caricature or one stereotype. If we could only do that, if we could only juxtapose in broad and expansive ways as do our children, we might see the sins of our prejudice and we might find our hearts opening up to those who might have otherwise never entered the circle of our care.

In Ken Burns' television series on the Civil War, the narrator describes a remarkable scene that took place in 1913 on the fiftieth anniversary of the Battle of Gettysburg. What was left of the two armies decided to stage a re-enactment of Picket's charge. All the old Union veterans took their place among the rocks on the ridge and the old Confederate veterans started marching toward them across the field below. And then something remarkable happened. As the old men among the rocks began to rush down at the old men coming across the field, a great cry went up. Only this time, instead of doing battle as they did half a century earlier, they threw their arms around each other, and they embraced and openly wept. In the original battle, they juxtaposed the persons on the other side of the hill with the enemy, the evil monsters which war makes them out to be. Now they juxtaposed correctly. They saw the enemy as someone like themselves, someone who shared in all the hurts and pains and joys which life happens to bring. They wept because they may have realized that had they juxtaposed that way in 1863, maybe there wouldn't have had to be a war where so many beautiful and innocent people were killed.

And that makes you wonder about the people whom we label as our enemy, whom we despise because of something they did to us. If we could see them as those old veterans saw each other, if we could juxtapose correctly, if we could see how those we are at war with share the same hurts and pains as we do, maybe we'd look upon them differently. Maybe we'd find that what is so bad about them is precisely the same thing that so many people find to be bad about us. Juxtaposing correctly might not only help us see the sin of prejudice but also see the sin of our private little wars. Juxtaposing correctly opens many a heart.

It also opens many a mind. Abraham Maslow once observed the following: give an adult a hammer and all he uses it for is to pound nails. Give a child a hammer and he dig withs it, sculpts with it, weighs down papers with leaves in between, knocks down apples, all sorts of things. The difference lies in the fact that nobody told the child that the purpose of the hammer is to hit a nail. The child juxtaposed the hammer with all sorts of possibilities.

As I mentioned earlier, children juxtapose much more broadly than do adults, so it really isn't any wonder as to why researchers tell us that the most creative people in the world are the children under five. They're not locked onto one or two pictures as to how things are supposed to be used, as to how things are supposed to be done. By not juxtaposing as narrowly as we adults juxtapose, they're open to a myriad of possibilities of doing things or using things, possibilities often absent in the thinking of many adults.

I remember reading of a tractor-trailer wedged under a bridge. No one could figure how to set it free. Engineers and experts converged upon the scene and they considered cutting off its top or perhaps pulling it free with bulldozers. In the midst of all their deliberations, a young boy happened to come by and said to the engineer: "Why don't you just let some air out of the tires?"

Because those adult experts were juxtaposing so narrowly, they didn't see the easy solution a child happened to see. Juxtaposing correctly may not only help us see the sin of prejudice or the sin of war, but it may also help us take note of the narrow-mindedness so common to us all. There's a lot to be found and discovered and created thanks to juxtaposing correctly. So juxtaposing opens a lot of hearts, it opens a lot of minds, and it also opens a lot of wills.

I'm reminded here of two outstanding athletes: Donny Moore of the California Angels and Chris Weber of the Washington Bullets. In 1986, Donny Moore was the eighth relief pitcher in a game that was to decide the representative of the American League in the World Series. If he put out the batter he faced, victory would be theirs. Unfortunately, the batter got ahold of his fast ball and sent it over the fence for a home run, costing the California Angels the championship and a trip to the World Series. Donny Moore never recovered from that pitch or that day and a few years later he tragically took his own life.

Chris Weber shared a similar story to that of Donny Moore except his sport was basketball, not baseball. He played on the Michigan team in the game that was to decide the NCAA championship. He called time-out in the waning seconds only to discover, to his chagrin, that his team's allotment of time-outs had already been used. His gaffe cost Michigan possession of the ball and with it the National Championship. Unlike Moore, however, he recovered from his mistake and in the following year went on to become the NBA Rookie of the Year.

The difference between Moore and Weber rested in the juxtaposition of their mistakes. Moore juxtaposed his with shame, depression, and other mistakes while Weber juxtaposed his with the success he had previously experienced. Weber was in touch with the reality of failure as an integral part of life. Unfortunately, that was not the case with Moore. The will to live, the will to go on with life, the will to achieve what we're capable of achieving is directly commensurate to how we juxtapose success and failure. To do so correctly, as evidenced by Weber, makes all the difference in the world.

I've been talking about juxtaposing because I see our Scriptures today doing so when it comes to God. The beginning of our first reading has God bearing this image of a mean and angry and vindictive individual bent on destroying us, an image held strongly by many believers. Next to that bogus image is attached the true image of God which the second reading describes as "rich in mercy and full of kindness," a God whom the Gospel describes as "having so loved the world that he gave his only begotten Son, that whoever believes in him may not perish but may have eternal life." When we hearers of the Word are filled with an overwhelming sense of sin, when we think ourselves unworthy of any kind of love, that's the image of God we need to juxtapose to our experience.

Juxtaposing correctly can help put an end to prejudice, it can help expose the folly of our private little wars, it can strike a blow to our narrow-mindedness, it can help overcome defeatism, but most especially it can help pull down the barriers between God's love and us. Bless yourself, bless others this Lenten day by looking at how you juxtapose when you experience life and when you experience people. Juxtapose as children do, juxtapose broadly, and you'll help create a world where less frequent will be the incidence of alienation and prejudice and war and small-mindedness and suicide.

Nevertheless

Scripture Lesson: 1 Corinthians 1:22-25
*... Christ crucified, a stumbling block to Jews,
an absurdity to Gentiles ...*

A Lenten message hailing the practice of ignoring conventional
wisdom, common thinking, and societal expectation.

Henrik Ibsen, the Norwegian dramatist, was a great critic of
the society in which he lived. He was also a great debater. The
story goes that he met his death while in the midst of a debate. Just
as he was giving his rebuttal to what had previously been said, he
got out the word "nevertheless." It was at that point, while mouthing that word, that Henrik Ibsen fell to his death, the apparent victim of a heart attack.

When I read that little piece from Ibsen's biography, I couldn't
help but think how fitting it was that "nevertheless" be his last
word, for here was someone who loved to counter what were often
the prevailing points of view of the society of his day. And as I
thought further, I couldn't help but think how fitting is the word
"nevertheless" when it comes to the people of God. If you think of
it, people of God, people who inspire and uplift the world, often
lead a life that runs counter to the prevailing points of view of the
society in which they live.

It could be those following the gospel of Jesus Christ or it could
be those helping to reveal to the world the glory that is God's.
What you'll find is that conventional wisdom, common thinking,
societal expectation dictated to them a certain way of being and
behaving yet, nevertheless, they chose another way; yet, nevertheless, they walked a different path. The word nevertheless can be
found amidst the descriptions of many great and inspiring people.

Beethoven grew deaf; nevertheless he continued to compose
music. Milton was blind; nevertheless he continued to write poetry.
Helen Keller was both blind and deaf; nevertheless she contributed

greatly to this world. Glenn Cunningham, at the age of three, was told he would never walk again; nevertheless he broke the world's record for the mile in 1934. Max Cleland lost both legs and an arm in Vietnam; nevertheless he became a U.S. Senator. Franklin Roosevelt was struck down by infantile paralysis; nevertheless he became president. Grandma Moses was eighty years old; nevertheless she began a career in painting.

One night the evening news reported that a young man was receiving his Eagle Scout award. Nothing noteworthy about that except that he was 22 and couldn't give his acceptance speech. His father spoke for him using the words his son was forming as he pointed to letters on a board atop his wheelchair. The young man I'm referring to had cerebral palsy; nevertheless he earned his merit badge in hiking, by pushing his wheelchair nine miles, then crawling the rest of the way.

That news report reminded me of the Academy Award-winning film *My Left Foot*. It starred Daniel Day-Lewis as Christy Brown, a true-to-life character who, against impossible odds, found a way to use his horribly disabled body to paint and to write. He could move only his toe and a part of his foot; nevertheless Christy Brown created beauty and made something of his life.

I could go on until tomorrow with example after example of people who move our hearts, who inspire us, who lift us up, not just because of what they accomplished but more so because those accomplishments were had despite being physically challenged, despite obstacles standing in their way. Although these heroic individuals were struck down by one of life's many injustices, nevertheless they carried on with life, nevertheless they chose not to allow the injustice to keep them from expressing their talent and making a contribution to this world. Although society might label them useless and call them a liability, nevertheless they went out and proved those labels wrong. Although their condition dictated their acting and behaving in a certain way, nevertheless they chose another path and in so doing they gave glory and honor to God.

During a recent Christmas break, I got a chance to see a few movies. The one that really moved me starred Daniel-Day Lewis, the same actor who played Christy Brown. The movie I'm referring to is called *The Crucible*, a film rendition of the great Arthur Miller play[1] based on the Salem witch trials. John Proctor, the lead character, has been persuaded to lie, to admit that he saw the devil and then bound himself to the devil's service. It was part of a plea bargain to save his life. But when the court had him sign his confession, intending to post it publicly for all to see, Proctor tore it up and renounced his confession. He couldn't put his name to a lie. Although he knew the court would now have to sentence him to die, nevertheless he held firm to the truth and marched proudly to the gallows.

John Proctor was a fictional character but he represents people throughout history and people of these present times who refuse to allow certain circumstances to excuse the selling of their souls. We've seen it in prisoner of war camps, we've seen it in Congress, in Tiananmen Square China, in the midst of the Holocaust, in corporate board rooms. People have had freedom or power or money or a stay of execution dangled before them in exchange for a simple yes or a simple no but they wouldn't provide it. They wouldn't stray from their principles or beliefs. They held fast to the truth and, in some cases like John Proctor's, it cost them their very life.

In light of the circumstances, conventional wisdom would have advised that a little lie would be perfectly all right. Common thinking would have it that no fault could be assigned if they acquiesced to the yes or the no. Society would even go so far as to say they'd be foolish not to follow that wisdom or that thinking. All that being said, nevertheless they did what they did; nevertheless they gave up freedom and they gave up power and in some cases they gave up their very life. Those special men and women stand tall today because although they could have lied and been spared pain and misery and unemployment and even death, nevertheless they held to the truth and in so doing they gave honor and glory to God.

On a cold night in February, a decade or so ago, 27-year-old Paul Keating was walking home in Manhattan's Greenwich Village when he saw two armed muggers robbing a college student. Keating, a gentle and much admired photographer for *Time* magazine, had every reason to avoid trouble. He didn't know the student. No one knew he saw them. He was outnumbered. He had

27

everything to lose and nothing to gain by getting involved; nevertheless he did. He confronted the muggers. The college student escaped and ran to a deli for help. A few moments later, two shots rang out. The muggers fled and Paul Keating was found dead on the street.

Now, you can call that an isolated story, an isolated incident, but the story and incident are repeated often in life. Many have walked in the shoes of Paul Keating. The situation may not have been as dire. It may not have been life threatening. But it was a situation where someone was in trouble, where help was needed, and they could have chosen not to get involved. They could have easily slipped away. They could have said: "It's not my responsibility!" Nevertheless, they got involved; they stopped and helped. Common thinking, conventional wisdom, and society itself would have cautioned against it, claiming that it wasn't the smartest or wisest thing to do. Nevertheless, they did it. Nevertheless, they stuck out their necks and unfortunately in some cases, like Paul Keating, they paid the ultimate price. They gave their very life.

When you think about it, the word nevertheless is the word of heroes. It's the word of practitioners of unbelievable courage. It's the word of those who stand out from the rest of society because they do what isn't expected; they do what isn't required; they do what could have easily been excused away. The word nevertheless is linked to those who, by standing out from the crowd, by defying conventional wisdom and common thinking, give honor and glory to God.

Along the coast of the Atlantic Ocean, there lived an old man. Every day when the tide went out he would make his way along the beach for miles. Another man who lived not far away would occasionally watch as the old man vanished into the distance and then later he'd notice that he returned. The neighbor also noticed that, as he walked, the old man would often swoop down to lift something from the sand and then toss it far away into the ocean. One day, when the old man went down to the beach, this neighbor out of curiosity followed him hoping to determine just what he happened to be doing. The neighbor saw that the old man was picking up starfish that had been stranded by the retreating tide and would die of dehydration before the tide returned. As the old man turned to return a starfish to the ocean, the neighbor called out with a degree of mockery in his voice: "Hey! Old Timer! What are you doing? This beach goes on for hundreds of miles and thousands of starfish get washed up every day. Surely you don't think that throwing a few back is going to matter!" The old man listened, paused for a moment, then taking the starfish in his hand and hurling it to the sea, he said to his neighbor: "It matters to this one!"

The word "nevertheless" isn't just reserved for heroes and for people of unbelievable courage. It's a word that describes a lot of plain and ordinary people who, in their small corner of life, are doing something that seems pretty small, who are doing something that may even seem useless, as though it's hardly going to matter. It could be a small act of kindness. It could be a small token of thoughtfulness. It could be a display of generosity. It could be the assuming of a responsibility that nobody wants to assume. What makes it special, what puts it in the league of tributes to the honor and glory of God, is that it doesn't have to be done. It isn't required. It could easily be excused away. But, nevertheless, the sacrifice is made; nevertheless, the deed is done; nevertheless, the action is performed. And lest it be, like that old man, lest it be criticized as the doing of something which in the big picture doesn't really matter, just remember, it matters to the one on the receiving end and ultimately it matters to God.

The word "nevertheless" is a word associated with the likes of a Beethoven or a Milton or a Glenn Cunningham or Paul Keating. But it's also a word associated with ordinary people like you and me who in small and quiet ways do what is unexpected, do what is not in league with conventional wisdom, common thinking, and usual practice. Engaging in such behavior not only gives honor and glory to God, but it's reflective of God's relationship with us.

That's the point of this sermon. That's the point of the Lenten season. Over these forty days from Ash Wednesday to Easter, we're reflecting on the life of Christ who reveals to all of us the magnitude of God's love, a magnitude measured by the word "nevertheless," a magnitude which Saint Paul describes today as a stumbling block for Jews, an absurdity to Gentiles.

Jesus tells us that although we may be undeserving of God's love, nevertheless that love is given. Although we're undeserving of God's forgiveness, nevertheless God forgives us. Although we're undeserving of God's attention, nevertheless he counts every hair on our head. Although we've let God down, although we act and behave contrary to God's will, nevertheless God's love is unconditional, it knows no bounds.

In a graveyard in Edinburgh, Scotland, there's the grave of the little daughter of Sir James Simpson, a scientist of great renown. On her tombstone are carved her name and along with it the words: "Nevertheless, I live!" The essence of this Lenten season is captured in the words: "God so loved the world that he gave his only begotten son, that whoever believes in him may not perish but have eternal life." We may not think we're worthy of God's love, nevertheless it's been given. And when we reach the end of our life, "nevertheless" may not be, like Henrik Ibsen, the last word we speak but it will definitely be the last word because although we may die, nevertheless we live.

---

1. Arthur Miller, *The Crucible: A Play in Four Acts* (London: Secker & Warburg, 1966).

Top Ten List

Scripture Lesson: Luke 14:1, 7-14
"... For everyone who exalts himself will be humbled ..."

An encore presentation from my previous book.

From time to time, I've used a bit from *The David Letterman Show* as a backdrop for a homily, in particular his Top Ten List. In the past, I've presented a Top Ten List of why we need to practice forgiveness as well as one on the top ten leading causes of blindness.

With today's Gospel centering around the theme of humility, I thought I might do another Top Ten List, this time presenting the top ten reasons why we need to practice humility. So bear with me now as I, in Letterman fashion, count down from 10 to 1.

Reason Number 10 is that it can save us from embarrassment. I like the story of the Army major who was sitting in his brand new office when a private appeared at his door. To impress the private, the major said: "Come in, soldier, I will be right with you after I answer this phone call." Speaking into the phone he said: "Well, General, it is good to hear your voice. How can I help you?" A pause followed and then the major said: "Fine, General, I will call the President within the hour." Having completed the call, he said to the private: "Now, soldier, what can I do for you?" The private, who had been staring at the floor nervously said in a low voice: "The sergeant told me to come in here and hook up your telephone."

So often, when we put on airs, when we pretend to be greater and smarter and more important than we really are, it is almost inevitable that people will see through the facade. People will come to realize that we are not all that we made ourselves out to be. So rather than endure that type of embarrassment, it would do us well to practice a little humility and be more honest when it comes to our talents and abilities and our state in life.

Reason Number 9 as to why we need to practice humility is that it is an avenue to healing. The word "shenanigan" is an Irish word and its roots come from a legend concerning the shee. The shee were invisible little people who were noted for such spiritual pranks as making tables dance and pots and pans rumble. According to the legend, they staged those pranks, known as shenanigans, to let humans know that contrary to how they thought and felt, they were not in total control of everything.

One of the by-products of humility is that very point. It is the realization that we are not in control of everything; contrary to what we like to think, there are certain things we can't handle. People who are alcoholic, people who are addicted to drugs, people who overeat or gamble excessively can never hope to be healed unless they come to that same conclusion. The reason why AA works or Gamblers Anonymous works is that those who attend the meetings have become humble enough and courageous enough to admit there is something they cannot handle, that there is something beyond their control.

Reason Number 8 as to why we need to practice humility is the reality of our indebtedness. A man once asked a surgeon: "How do you do it? With life and death in your hands, there you are all alone!" The surgeon replied: "I do not go into the operating room alone. Louis Pasteur goes with me, Joseph Lister goes with me, Michael De Bakey goes with me, Hippocrates goes with me."

William Marconi claimed that his epic-making discoveries would have been impossible had it not been for the experimenters before him, especially a humble and unknown scientist named Tay. David Livingston always attributed his success in Africa to his faithful and devoted African companions who accompanied him on expedition after expedition.

Anyone who has achieved anything in life — any surgeon, scientist, inventor, or what have you — owes a huge amount of debt not only to those who have gone before them but also to those who nurtured them and raised them and supported them.

I heard once of an agronomist who used a computer to analyze all the components involved in the growing of a record wheat crop. His conclusion was that God and the universe provided about 95 percent of the energies needed for the growth, while the farmer accounted for about five percent. So we all need to be humble in the face of what we have done and accomplished because it would not have happened were it not for our friends, our predecessors, our families — not to mention our eternal God.

Reason Number 7 as to why we need to practice humility is that we are not perfect. I just read recently that the architect of the Taj Mahal explicitly designed the magnificent building to have one minor flaw, and that was a tiny leak in the roof. The architect purposely put that flaw in the structure to remind humans that only God is capable of perfection.

Although we may be constantly reminded of that truth, some of us still, unfortunately, believe that perfection is within our means and because we can't humbly admit that it is not, we make life miserable for ourselves and everyone around us.

I like the statement I found in a magazine that went: "If you suddenly gained the muscle power of 100 men and could out-wrestle King Kong, it does not mean that you still wouldn't have to worry about dandruff, acne, or hemorrhoids."

Reason Number 6 as to why we need to practice humility is that most truly great individuals do. A young American student visiting the Beethoven museum was fascinated by the piano on which Beethoven had composed some of his greatest works. She asked the museum guard if she could sit where Beethoven sat and play a few bars on the piano. She accompanied her request with a lavish tip. The man agreed. The girl sat down at the piano and tinkled out the opening of the "Moonlight Sonata." As she was leaving, she said to the guard: "I suppose all the great pianists who come here want to play that piano!" The guard shook his head. "Paderewski was here a few years ago and he said he wasn't even worthy to touch its keys!"

It's interesting to note how so many of those who will go down in history as truly great individuals have been heavily endowed with humility. They not only realize their indebtedness to so many but they have the sense that they are mere instruments for the glory of God. They believe that the power and talents that ushered forth their greatest work and their most magnificent of creations were given to them and not created by them. If we wish to be looked upon as great, we need to practice humility.

Reason Number 5 as to why we need to practice humility is that it can save us from getting hurt. There is an Aesop fable about a group of mice who decided that they needed to be better organized. So they elected some leaders who immediately initiated several changes. The leaders devised innovative ways to find food and creative ways to escape from the house cat. All in the mouse kingdom were pleased and happy. But then as time went along, the mice leaders became more and more caught up in their own self-importance. They said: "We are the leaders here, we should have titles and privileges. We should wear handsome uniforms with lots of medals and tall hats too so that, when we pass by, everyone will recognize us immediately and give us the respect we deserve." So they did just that. They put on the uniforms and medals and tall hats and they looked good and they felt very proud. Then one day the cat launched a surprise attack. All the mice ran for their lives. The mice leaders were so weighed down by their numerous, heavy medals that they could not run fast. But, even worse, when they reached the escape hatch, they couldn't enter because their hats were too tall. The hungry cat had a sumptuous feast that day.

Whenever we get taken up by our own self-importance, whenever good pride gives way to arrogance, haughtiness, and pompousness, slowly but surely, our friends will drift away, we'll no longer command respect, and it won't be long before a feeling of emptiness arises. In essence, when we fail to practice humility, like those mice, we are setting ourselves up for disaster; we are setting ourselves up for getting hurt.

Reason Number 4 as to why we need to practice humility is that but for the grace of God, go we. I remember hearing a lecture in which the speaker, whose name escapes me, said that whenever tragedy strikes, whenever bad things come, we ask the wrong question. We ask: "Why me?" when we should be asking, "Why not me?" The lecturer queried as to whether our tragedy or bad thing should have gone to the woman next door who has five kids or whether it should have gone to the kid down the street who is ten years old. In essence, he asked: "What makes us more undeserving of a bad break than someone else?"

The lecture, I believe, hit on something that rings true for far too many of us, and that's this notion that we are somewhat better than most people, that we deserve the breaks we get, that the blessings we have are a product of our merit and not a product of God's grace. The truth, of course, is otherwise. A strong dose of humility can help us see that, as far as the recipient of a bad break goes, but for the grace of God go we.

Reason Number 3 as to why we need to practice humility is that it can positively change our life. One of the most loved of all movies is *The Wizard of Oz*. Whenever we reference that movie, our attention centers on Dorothy, the scarecrow, the lion, and the tin man. The one character we often forget is the Wizard himself. The Wizard, like Dorothy and company, also undergoes a positive transformation.

You might recall how he falsely presented himself as a powerful individual, a mighty fear-inspiring force, a legendary sage, and then, thanks to Dorothy's dog, his false facade came tumbling down and he was exposed as a fraud.

That humiliation proved to work a blessing because the Wizard was forced to be himself and, as a result, changed into an honest, happy, humble man. He found life to be far more enjoyable than it had been when he portrayed himself as someone he was not. The practice of humility carries with it the virtue of honesty which enables people to see us as we really are, thus eliminating the inner turmoil that accompanies our pretense and our acting. Those who practice humility live a far happier and far less anxious life than those who do not.

Reason Number 2 as to why we need to practice humility is that, contrary to what we may think, we do not know everything. I like the story of a student who burst forth from his graduation ceremony and cried: "Here I am world, I have a B.A.!" And the world replied: "Well, stick around, son, stick around, daughter, and I will teach you the rest of the alphabet!" It was Harry Truman who said: "It is what you learn after you know it all that really counts."

Far too many of us have this prideful notion that we know everything, that we know it all and, if that is our belief, then no one can teach us or tell us anything. Humility enables us to recognize the many gaps in our knowledge and makes us, therefore, eager and open to new ideas, new thoughts, and new insights into life.

Finally, and here is where Antoine of the Letterman show does his drum roll, **Reason Number 1** as to why we need to practice humility is that Jesus practiced it as well. A Christian leader visiting in China asked a group of Chinese pastors what it was in Christ that appealed to them most and won their hearts. Nobody mentioned the miracles or even the Sermon on the Mount. Some of the elders, in a choking, faltering voice, said: "It was the story of the upper room when Christ washed the disciples' feet." Jesus Christ, who had all the reasons to lord it over all, chose instead to be a servant. He practiced humility and asked us to do the same.

So there you have it, the top ten reasons why we should practice humility. Suffice it to say, if you haven't done so, perhaps it is time you began.

Stinkin Thinkin

Scripture Lesson: Matthew 16:21-27
"... Get behind me, Satan!
You're not thinking as God but as Man ..."

An accounting of some thinking that doesn't quite make the grade when it comes to God.

———————————

Alcoholics Anonymous has a phrase they use when people are thinking in a way that not only fails to connect with reality but perpetuates, as well, certain myths not compatible with truth. The phrase I am referring to is: "stinkin thinkin." "Stinkin thinkin" is not something particular to the alcoholic; it's something of which all of us are guilty. Rare is the person who has not done his or her share of "stinkin thinkin."

I reference that phrase because it fits the thoughts of Peter in today's Gospel. When he interrupts Jesus, taking issue with his references to pain and suffering, Jesus explodes with the famous line: "Get behind me, Satan! You're not thinking as God but as Man." In essence, he was accusing Peter of thinking in terms of fantasy; he was accusing Peter of "stinkin thinkin."

That being said, I thought I'd talk with you today about how we participate in that kind of thinking. I would like to talk with you about some matters and thoughts pertaining to God that could easily qualify as "stinkin thinkin."

Consider the belief that God punishes sinners. William Barclay, the great British biblical scholar, was on a vacation in Ireland. One afternoon his daughter and son-in-law went sailing only to perish in a sudden squall. Soon after, Professor Barclay received an anonymous letter telling him that God had drowned his dear ones to get even with him for his heretical teaching.

Jacqueline Dupre, the cellist, was afflicted with multiple sclerosis. One of the terrible things she had to contend with was her mother and her friend who were fundamentalists. They kept telling her that she got multiple sclerosis because she had given up her nominal Christian faith to marry someone who is Jewish.

I will never forget a friend who tragically lost her baby to a long illness. When I saw her in church the following Sunday, she said to me: "Father, maybe if I would have come to church more often, God would not have taken my child!"

I know of someone who was in tremendous turmoil because she was diagnosed with cancer. What was really the source of her torment was that earlier in her life she had slept with someone to whom she was not married and she believed her cancer was God's way of getting back at her for her sin.

When the floods hit the Midwest several years ago, floods that inflicted horrible damage on many cities, a poll was taken and eighteen percent of those polled believe that God sent those floods as punishment for peoples' sins. Though I've not seen poll numbers in regards to it, I am afraid that there are a great many who believe the AIDS virus was created by God as punishment for homosexuality.

To believe that a God of love is behind such horrible things as cancer and MS and AIDS as well as the death of babies is not only preposterous but also downright blasphemous. To suggest that a God of justice would pick on a small-time sinner and somehow leave the Adolf Hitlers, the Stalins, and the Slobodan Milosevics unscathed is ridiculous. To believe that God punishes people with tragedy is "stinkin thinkin." To believe life is fair and people get what they deserve is "stinkin thinkin." To believe, as so many of my patients in the hospital believe, that they must have done something wrong to be as sick as they are is "stinkin thinkin."

And along a similar track is the belief that though God might not punish sinners, the bad things of life are all part of God's will.

William Sloane Coffin lost a son very tragically. While driving home one night in a blinding rainstorm, he lost control of his car and drove into the Boston River where he drowned. When word got to Coffin, as you might imagine, he was beside himself with grief. One of his friends, in an effort to console him, said those awful words: "It must have been God's will!" This prompted a stunning rebuke on the part of Coffin. He said: "Do you think it was the will of God that my son never fixed that lousy windshield wiper? Do you think it was the will of God that there were no streetlights on that stretch of road and no guardrail separating it from the river?" William Sloane Coffin then uttered a line I have quoted many times. He said: "My consolation over my son's death lies in knowing that it was not the will of God that he died but that, when the waves closed over his sinking car, God's heart was the first of all of our hearts to break!"

When it comes to so many of the bad and tragic things of life, I believe that the Hindu Saint Swami Ramdas had the proper handle on it. Someone told him about an agnostic who said that if he believed in God, he would strangle him for the all the suffering he has caused in the world. The Swami said in reply that if he met that man he would place the man's hands around the man's own neck and throat and say: "Here is the one who is causing the suffering, strangle him!"

So much of the evil in our world, so much of the world's pain and suffering is not God made but, pardon the language, man made. The basis of so much that is wrong with the world is hatred and greed and selfishness and bigotry and prejudice and envy and apathy and the other assorted sins of which, I'm afraid, we're all guilty. Pain and suffering are not products of God's will but products of human will. To believe that pain and suffering are God's doing is "stinkin thinkin." To believe that when tragedy strikes it must have been God's will is "stinkin thinkin."

And right alongside this notion of God's being responsible for all the bad things of life, there is also the notion of God's being responsible for everything in this life, the notion that nothing really matters because all of life has been scripted in advance by God.

The story is told of two rabbis, Rabbi Ishmael and Rabbi Akiba. Walking along the streets of ancient Rome, they came upon a sick man lying by the side of the road. They saw in the distance a farmer plowing his field. Rabbi Ishmael called to the farmer and asked that he go quickly to the nearest town and summon a physician. The farmer refused the rabbi's request saying it would be a waste of time to do it. He said: "If God had planned for the man to live, he would. If he planned for the man to die, he will die. Summoning a physician, therefore, is of no use." The rabbi, angered by such thinking, said: "What do you have in your hand?" The man answered: "A plow, of course!" The rabbi then said: "Why do you interfere with the earth that God has created? If God planned for your crops to grow, they will grow. If God planned for your crops not to grow, they won't grow. But here you are plowing and watering and weeding. If getting a physician is a waste of time, so is your plowing and watering and weeding."

As it is for the farmer and physician, so it is for us. We, not God, bear ultimate responsibility for the kind of world in which we live. Although God is in control of the waters, we steer the ship and the direction of that ship has not been predestined or predetermined. Our destiny is in our hands and it rests on how we make use of the plow God has given us to use.

One of my favorite Anthony De Mello stories involves a woman who dreams she walked into a store and to her surprise found God behind the counter. "What do you sell here?" she asked. "Everything your heart desires!" said God. Hardly daring to believe what she was hearing, the woman decided to ask for the best things a human being could desire. "I want peace of mind, love and happiness and wisdom and freedom from fear!" she said. Then, as an afterthought, she added: "Not just for me but for everyone on earth!" God smiled and laughed and said: "I think you have it all wrong, my dear, we don't sell fruits here. We sell only seeds!"

This Machiavellian notion that God is up above pulling all of our strings is "stinkin thinkin." The idea that God has everything scripted, that we have all been predestined and predetermined is "stinkin thinkin." To believe that God is going to hand us life on a platter, that he will give us fruit instead of seed, is "stinkin thinkin." Always keep in mind that wonderful story where a man is complaining because God has done nothing to alleviate poverty or help the poor and God replies with a smile: "I have done something. I created you."

And, finally, when it comes to "stinkin thinkin," you have the notion that certain credentials are required of those who wish to enter God's Kingdom.

I learned recently that, at an assembly of the Presbyterian Church several years back, one of the matters for discussion was a long held piece of doctrine which stated that anyone who was not baptized was automatically excluded from God's Kingdom. After several hours of debate, it was finally decided a change was in order. A polling of the assembly resulted in the passing of a motion declaring the importance of baptism but also recognizing the reality that the unbaptized also had access to salvation. Having resolved the doctrinal matter, the head of the assembly moved on to new business only to notice a hand up in the back of the room. Inquiring about the nature of his request, the individual in question said he wished to make a new motion. He said: "Since the Presbyterian Church has just recognized that God's grace is now open to the unbaptized, I wish to make a motion that the new doctrine be made retroactive."

We can laugh at the story (we Catholics, by the way, were not much different from the Presbyterians), but there are still many who believe that God's favor has limits. There are many who believe that only certain religions and faiths have access to God's Kingdom. There are many that believe God's love is limited, that God only loves Christians! It's all an example and a matter of "stinkin thinkin."

When you examine all the points I've raised today, you'll find that behind our "stinkin thinkin" is what's behind Peter's "stinkin thinkin." We are thinking like men and women and not thinking like God. We believe God to be vindictive as we are, to be mean-spirited as we are, to be hard and tough as nails as we are, a control freak, and very prejudiced and as narrow-minded as we are. As Jesus told us through his life and his parables, God is a God of love and mercy and compassion. To think of God in any other way is "stinkin thinkin."

Anonymous

Scripture Lesson: 1 Corinthians 10:16-17
... we, many though we are, are one body ...

The feast of Corpus Christi gives us cause to remember not only the wideness of God's family but also the truth of the importance of every member of that family.

If you were to compose a list of the top ten poets or the top ten writers of all time there's one person heading both lists. That person is responsible for warming billions of hearts and getting billions to lift their voices to the heavens above. All of you here have sung that person's songs, you've read some of that person's poetry. That same person has authored stories that I've told and read as well as stories you've told and read. I'm talking about the woman or man known as Anonymous.

Every hymnbook will list at least 25 hymns to the credit of that unknown person, likewise for every book of poetry, likewise for every book of stories. Listen to some of the entries credited to that wonderful individual. There's the Old English narrative poem *Beowulf.* There's the often-read play *Everyman.* There are those beloved Christmas carols, "Adeste Fidelis," "The Twelve Days Of Christmas," and "Jolly Old St. Nicholas." Michael Flatley is dancing up a storm these days with a song called "Lord Of The Dance." That song is really titled "Simple Gifts" and the author is Anonymous. We've all sung "The Strife Is O'er, The Battle Done." We've said the "Hail Mary" many times. I could go on and on until tomorrow with songs and prayers and poems and stories, all of which came from a writer whose name is unknown and who has long since been forgotten.

Consider, as well, some of the greatest inventions of all time. There are things that have greatly benefited humankind and we have no idea who was ultimately responsible for their discovery. There are a lot of gods and goddesses, for example, associated with the gift of fire, but as far as human beings are concerned there's no one to whom we can credit the idea of rubbing two sticks together to make a flame. Or how about the wheel or the lever or how about silk or wool? There's no name associated with their discovery except the person called Anonymous.

Or take what I have tabbed as the greatest discovery of this century: cardiopulmonary resuscitation, the art of compressions to the chest and mouth-to-mouth breathing. There's probably a surgeon associated with its predecessor, the open heart massage, but there's no individual, to my knowledge, whom we can cite as the one who practically converted that grisly surgical intervention into something which ordinary people could do. The world of invention and discovery is filled with all kinds of gadgets, procedures, and products of nature which have come our way via the one known as Anonymous.

Consider the New Testament. How many of those who served greatly the cause of Christ were without name? There was the man, for instance, in our Gospel today who was carrying the water jar and who told of the man who provided the room where the Last Supper was held. We do not have their names but they were a vital part of one of the greatest days in the life of Christ and ultimately our lives as well. Or how about the town clerk in Ephesus who saved the life of Saint Paul by a flash of common sense amidst confusion? We know his position, but not his name. Literally thousands of figures, not just in the New Testament but in the Old Testament, as well, factored greatly and critically in Salvation History. They are individuals known as Anonymous.

Then you have those who have left their mark on life but not as dramatically or as notably as those I've just mentioned. I'm reminded of the scene that took place at the burial of the poet Longfellow. A notable company gathered at the funeral, among them Ralph Waldo Emerson who had come up from Concord. He, too, was up in age. He stood for a long, long time staring down at the quiet, dead face of Longfellow but he said nothing. At last he turned sadly away and, as he did so, he remarked to those who stood reverently by: "The gentleman we're burying today was a sweet and beautiful soul, but I'm afraid I've already forgotten his name." Now Longfellow was lucky because, although Emerson forgot his name, others didn't and Longfellow ranks among the greatest in literature. But down through the years I'm sure there have been many extremely talented people who might have been equal to or a greater than a Longfellow but, unfortunately for them, everyone has forgotten their names and they left no traces of their work for us to remember them. So they, too, rank amongst the anonymous but perhaps not as notably as far as history is concerned.

Besides all the writers and poets and inventors and discoverers and figures of scripture who share the moniker Anonymous and who have made their mark directly on life, there are those anonymous individuals who left their mark indirectly on life. I'm referring here to those who helped shape and mold the known greats of history. I'm referring to those who were a major influence in the life of someone who will forever be remembered because of what he or she achieved or accomplished.

There's a legend concerning a king who decided to set aside a special day to honor his greatest subject. When the big day arrived, there was a large gathering in the palace courtyard. Four finalists were brought forward; from these four the king would select the winner. The first person presented was a wealthy philanthropist. The king was told that this man was highly deserving of the honor because of his humanitarian efforts. He had given much of his wealth to the poor. The second person was a celebrated physician. The king was told that this doctor was highly deserving of the honor because he had rendered faithful and dedicated service to the sick for many years. The third person was a distinguished judge. The king was told the judge was worthy because he was noted for his wisdom, his fairness, and his brilliant decisions. The fourth person presented was an elderly woman. Everyone was quite surprised to see her there because her manner was quite humble, as was her dress. She hardly looked the part of someone who would be honored as the greatest subject in the kingdom. Everyone thought: "What chance could she possibly have when compared to the other three who had accomplished so much?" Even so, there was something about her, the look of love in her face, the understanding in her eyes, her quiet confidence. The king was intrigued, to say the least, and somewhat puzzled by her presence. He asked who she was. And the answer came: "You see the philanthropist, the doctor, and the judge. Well, she was their teacher."

Now, if you were to comb through the history of the movers and shakers from the past as well as the present, if you were to peruse the life stories of the very famous poets, inventors, and even famous figures of Sacred Scripture, you won't read who their teachers were, you may not even read who their parents were, and I'll bet that all and any who greatly influenced their work won't be mentioned either. But you can bet that the person, whose name will go into the history books or the Scriptures, wouldn't have amounted to anything without them.

Anonymous individuals have not only been responsible for great things and inspiring things on their own part; they've also been responsible for great things and inspiring things on the part of someone other than themselves. Those known individuals who will be or have been recorded in history because of their accomplishments owe a huge debt of gratitude to people who may have been known to them, but who will remain eternally anonymous to us.

And then, of course, there are all those people who may not have directly influenced someone great and famous but who instead did all the spade work necessary for greatness and notoriety to be achieved. Because he signed the Emancipation Proclamation, Abraham Lincoln will always be acknowledged as freeing the slaves. But, if truth were told, many anonymous people put their lives on the line to call attention to the evil of slavery. Many people were humiliated, harassed, and silenced because they dared attack an institution that provided a considerable profit for many an influential person. Many a slave was killed because he/she dared to protest his or her indentured status. They've long been forgotten, they'll forever remain anonymous, but without their sacrifice Abraham Lincoln would never have been able to sign the Emancipation Proclamation.

You can say the same thing for Martin Luther King, Jr., who spearheaded the Civil Rights Movement of the '60s. He's looked upon as a hero but, without those anonymous crowds of people who marched on Washington, without those anonymous individuals who risked their lives and gave their lives to register black voters in the South, I doubt if he would have accomplished what he ultimately did accomplish. If not for the Anonymous, Martin Luther King, Jr., may not have made our history books.

I've been touting for the past several minutes the accomplishments and the influence and the importance of those we call Anonymous because we're celebrating in essence their feast day. The Body of Christ encompasses all the people in this world and it encompasses the many generations of people who preceded them. Some of them are famous, some of them are saints, some of them will be recalled and known until the end of time, but the vast majority are anonymous and that includes you and me.

This feast of Corpus Christi, the celebration of the Body of Christ, lets us know that the Anonymous are as important as the famous. Those who are forgotten are as cherished as those who are remembered. In the eyes of God we are equally loved. We are all members of God's family; as such, every hair on our head has been counted. God knows us each by name whether we're famous or whether we're anonymous. So the anonymous are important not just for what they have contributed to the world, not just for the great and famous people they've inspired, not just for the spade work they've done to further important causes, they're important because they happen to be the major stockholders in the club called the Body of Christ.

Four travelers were recently at a conference at Chicago. They stayed talking too long and were late in arriving at the local train station. Grabbing their bags from the taxi, they ran to the platform. One of them in his haste knocked over a table in which a local boy had some apples for sale. Being late, not wanting to miss the train, they ran on, cleared the gate, and arrived at the train before the doors closed. As they were about to board the waiting train, one of them stopped and, instead of getting on the train, decided to go back and see if the little kid whose table they knocked over was all right. When he got there, he discovered that the boy was nine years old and blind. Some of the apples he had been selling were damaged. He helped the boy as best he could and then said to him:

"Here's ten dollars to cover the cost of whatever is damaged." As he walked away the boy called out after him: "Hey, mister, are you Jesus?"

Now, the boy didn't know the man, the man didn't know the boy, and chances are good that they'd never see each other again and would probably soon forget that the incident ever took place. But the question the boy posed could have been posed as well by the man and the answer would have been "Yes" on both counts because, you see, Jesus chose anonymity as the vehicle by which he would enter life again. He said he would come blind and poor and as the least of one's brothers and sisters and he would come as well as a stranger helping out a person in need. That incident at the Chicago train station — two anonymous individuals in an interchange of love and help — that's vintage Jesus working as he always does under the guise of anonymity.

So, my friends, the Anonymous are not only the backbone of what goes on and has gone on in life. The Anonymous are not just the stockholders in the Body of Christ. They are the incarnation of Jesus himself.

So don't fret if someone forgets your name. Don't fret that you never get the credit you deserve. Don't fret that no one really knows who you are. You're in great company. You're a vehicle for Jesus and you might even be the one responsible for the emergence of some man or woman who will some day become famous. On this Corpus Christi day, give thanks for all the anonymous people who make up the Body of Christ. Give thanks to the anonymous people who've been a big part of your life. Give thanks as well that, even though we won't make the history books, even though we'll forever be anonymous to the world, we are never anonymous when it comes to God. He knows us each by name.

Dorian Gray And Us

Scripture Lesson: Matthew 10:26-33
... Nothing is concealed that will not be revealed ...

No matter how hard we try to hide our dark side, it can't be concealed!

————————————

One of the most celebrated stories of all time is Oscar Wilde's *The Picture of Dorian Gray*[1]. Dorian Gray is a very handsome and dashing young man who had a flair for mesmerizing everyone he met. His picture hung over the fireplace in his home. It reflected well his captivating charm. There was one problem, however. Dorian Gray was not a good man. He led a hedonistic life. He corrupted women. He betrayed his friends and he exhibited few, if any, principles. He was beautiful on the outside but ugly on the inside.

The story revolved around his picture which slowly began to change. It slowly began to take on the ugliness inside him. At first he ignored it but later, as the portrait became more twisted, more sullen, and more repulsive, he tore it from the wall and hid it in the attic where it continued to mirror the decaying soul that lay beneath his physically attractive features. The story ends with his destroying the picture only to discover, to his horror, that its ugly and twisted image had been transferred to him.

I reference that Oscar Wilde classic today because I'd like to talk with you about our inability to hide what might be wrong inside us. I'd like to talk with you about the fact that the chickens do come home to roost, that whatever bad we might have inside us cannot truly or really be concealed. Just as Dorian Gray had a portrait which revealed his hidden self, so do we have indicators that just as effectively do much the same for us. We may think that our dark side is holed up neatly inside us, but more often than we'd like to think, it's not the case at all.

Several years ago, an interesting article by Lois Wyse[2] appeared in *Good Housekeeping* magazine. It listed some bits of advice for young women considering marriage, some helpful guidelines for finding a good husband. She said there are six ways to learn everything you need to know about a man before you decide to marry him.

First: Watch him drive in heavy traffic. Second: Play tennis with him. Third: Listen as he talks to his mother when he doesn't know you're listening. Fourth: See how he treats those who serve him — waiters, waitresses, service attendants, etc. Five: Notice how and for whom and for what he spends his money. Six: Look at his friends. Lois Wyse saw the six points as providing windows into a potential husband's heart, clues as to the possibility of a dark side not noticeable in the romantic exchanges that usually mark a courtship.

Dwight L. Moody once defined character as what a person is in the dark. When one looks from a distance, as Wyse suggests in her six points, one is really seeing a person behave in the dark. It's peering through the veil hiding a person's character.

Sometimes, darkness and distance isn't needed at all. Sometimes one's inner life sits out there for all to see. I know a teacher of little children who one day got an anonymous note from one of her fifth graders. She became very upset because the note read: "If you feel all right, will you please notify your face!"

There are many people, like that teacher, who do not realize how they telegraph their feelings, how they show their disgust, how they display their disinterest, or how they exhibit their meanness. They may believe that no one can see it, they may think that they're hiding it, but it's there on their faces for all to see.

Then you have the assorted illnesses and sickness and health problems that serve as revelations of an inner life that's not too nice, an inner life hidden from the public eye. The Bay of Naples is the habitat of a jellyfish called Medusa and a snail of the Nudibranch variety. When the snail is small, the jellyfish will swoop down and consume it only to have it lodge in the digestive tract, its shell keeping it from going any farther. Once there, the snail slowly begins to feed on the digestive tract and, if not expelled, it will eat the entire jellyfish.

Quite often the dark side within us acts like that snail. It eats away at our insides. The bitterness, the anger, the envy, the hate, the desire for vengeance, the hostility that we might be carefully hiding from public view slowly begin to take their toll on our health. They eventually air themselves out in the form of a disease, a sickness, or a problem with our health.

In a study at a medical school that extended over 25 years, 255 future physicians took a battery of psychological tests. Those who admitted to hostile feelings inside them, over the course of the 25 years, had a four times greater incidence of illness and six times the mortality. That's just one of countless other studies that provide some impressive statistics tying certain diseases to moral and emotional conflicts within a person's life.

When our dark side is submerged beneath our outer life, it often finds its way to the surface via a sickness or health problem or disease. And sometimes it finds its way to the surface via the behavior and health problems of the people around us and near us.

Dr. Ashley Montague, the noted anthropologist, once got up before an audience of physicians and nurses and asked a question. He asked: "How can you demonstrate a lack of love on an X-ray?" No one in the room knew the answer. Montague then explained that when children aren't loved they don't grow; the evidence for this is the denser lines that can be seen on an X-ray of their bones. They are indicators of periods of time when love was lacking and growth did not occur.

All too often, the sins of fathers or mothers or both, sins hidden from public view, make their way into the open through their children, not just in their bone structure but in their behavior as well. Many a child's negative behavior can be tied to the dark side of a parent.

I remember a judge in Philadelphia once commenting that in all his experiences of dealing with juvenile delinquents, kids in trouble with the law, never once did he see a father show any sign of affection for his child. These were fathers who were prominent people in the community. Many seemingly wonderful fathers have these children from hell. You have to wonder if there might have

51

been incidence of neglect or physical or sexual abuse that made those children that way.

Be it the lack of affection, be it neglect, be it abuse, horrid products of a parent's dark side, they may seemingly be hidden from public view but they do show themselves in the bone structure, the behavior, and the overall physical and mental health of those whom they're near.

So our inner life, our dark side, is revealed in our dark and distant activities; it is revealed through our face, revealed through illness or disease, revealed through the health problems and difficulties of those close and near, and revealed as well in the performance of our duties.

Years ago, on a talk show, the Amazing Kreskin asked several top sports figures and police officers to stand eight feet from a hanging tire tube and throw a ball through it. Each of them did so repeatedly with no problem at all. Then he had them think of the most upsetting, distressing, and traumatic experience they had ever gone through. When each of them was set with a memory of that bad experience, he had them repeat the exercise. Whereas before they threw the ball through the tire tube with ease, now they missed the tire completely and one of them actually threw the ball over his head and behind him.

That Kreskin demonstration proved how much of an effect just the recollection of a bad experience can have on a simple task. Just think of how ongoing feelings of bitterness and hatred and envy and anger can affect our behavior. We're kidding ourselves if we think that the negative pieces of ourselves that we hide from others don't register an effect on our jobs, on our duties, or in the carrying out of our daily lives.

When you come right down to it, Jesus in our Gospel was right on target when he said: "Nothing is concealed that will not be revealed nor secret that will not be known!" In effect, our inner life, which we might be going to great pains to hide, never really does get hidden. The fate of Dorian Gray is our fate.

Our call today is to bare our souls, to confess our sins, to own up to the dark side within us. For only by doing so can we realize the grace of God's forgiveness and thus begin to live a life where we'll have nothing to hide, a life where our inner and outer selves are one. My friends, heed that call today and spare your health, your children, your spouse, and your work from the dark side within you.

_____

1. Oscar Wilde, *The Picture of Dorian Gray* (New York: Modern Library, 1985).

2. Described by James W. Moore, *When You're a Christian, the Whole World Is From Missouri* (Nashville: Dimensions for Living, 1997), p. 71.

Powerful Babies

Scripture Lesson: Matthew 2:1-12
> *... on entering the house, found*
> *the child with Mary his mother ...*

Who would have thought that a child in a manger would yield such
an impact?

————————————

It may or may not have happened in December, author Brete
Harte does not say, but in a place called Roaring Camp a baby was
born who would significantly change the lives of the people living
there. Roaring Camp was a mining town inhabited strictly by men,
men who would make the Road Vultures on their worst day look
like choirboys. They were dirty. Four-letter words seemed to be
their only vocabulary. They were nasty. Disputes were settled by
gunfire and their surroundings were so filthy that even cockroaches
turned away in disgust.

The baby was born to Cherokee Sal, a woman who had drifted
into camp just prior to the birth of her child. She would unfortunately die during the birthing process. So to these raucous, dirty,
nasty men came the challenge and reality of caring for the baby.
They laid the child on some rags in a shoebox and immediately
realized that the box would not do for a baby that beautiful. So a
man was sent eighty miles on a mule to get a rosewood cradle, the
best money could buy. The cradle was bought and brought back to
the camp, but no sooner did they lay the baby in the cradle than it
became obvious that the rags lining the cradle would not do. So the
same man who made the purchase was sent back those eighty miles
to buy the daintiest and softest of lace he could find. But as the
baby lay in this new cradle with its most beautiful of lace, the men
noticed with dismay what they had never noticed before: the floor
was positively filthy. So they scrubbed the floor and it wasn't long
before that scrubbing revealed the need for paint on the walls and

the need to fix the windows and the need to purchase curtains that would be of the quality of the lace in the cradle.

With the baby needing rest, the men put a lid on their raucous behavior and they also curbed their use of four-letter words. Not wanting to scare the baby with their looks, they all began shaving and cleaning their clothing and looking more like men going to Sunday school than men working in the mines.

In the mythical town of Roaring Camp, a baby is born and the whole town undergoes a positive transformation. Dirty, nasty, foul-mouth men became model citizens and a filthy run-down ranch became a palace.

I've relayed to you a story from the imagination of novelist Bret Harte[1] because I would like to talk with you today about babies and, in particular, the impact they can have upon life. What happened in Roaring Camp might be the stuff of fiction, but time and time again a baby is born who wields tremendous power. A baby is born who makes a tremendously positive impact not just on a town but often on an entire world.

Long ago, in Egypt, a slave girl held in her arms a newborn baby boy for whom there seemed no hope that he would be allowed to live. So she framed for him a floating cradle and pushed him out upon the waters of the Nile hoping that somehow he would survive. In retrospect, a whole civilization lay in that cradle. That baby was named Moses. He grew up to be the man who would lead the people of Abraham into the Promised Land.

In our own country, when the forces of this union were starting to rise, when the rift between the North and the South was beginning to widen, out of a meeting in Kentucky a young frontiersman and his bride went to build a log cabin near Nolans Creek and in that cabin a baby was born. And you wonder what would have become of these United States had it not been for that baby who was none other than Abraham Lincoln, who weathered our country through a terrible Civil War and who immediately thereafter did what probably no one else would have done — treat the South not as a fallen enemy but as an equal partner in a noble future.

Yes, indeed, a baby can have a tremendous impact on life. Babies can exhibit all sorts of unbelievable transformational power, maybe not in the immediate sense like Roaring Camp, but often in the long sense in that they may grow up to be someone whom the world will forever remember and to whom the world will be forever indebted.

I am reminded of a story that Leonard Rabinhill[2] tells about a group of tourists who were visiting a picturesque village. As they walked past an old man sitting by the fence, one tourist asked in a patronizing way: "Were any great men or women born in the village?" The old man replied: "Nope, only babies!"

People who loom largest in history, people who are responsible for so many blessings, people who have left a positive and powerful mark on the world, all gently and quietly came into life as a baby and, for the most part, no one would have believed back then that they were destined for greatness.

Who, for example, in the fifteenth century thought that anything important happened when in Janua, Spain, a child was born unadvertised and unheralded? That child would ultimately open the door of the most amazing geographical expansion in history. Always when the world least expects it, some Christopher Columbus is being born to introduce a new era, to mark the beginning of a whole new chapter in the history of the world. So long as there are babies, you can never tell.

The year 1809, for example, was one of the most discouraging in human history. Napoleon was running roughshod over all of Europe. His battles and victories were the absorbing news of the day. I would think that many were weary of the bloodshed, probably suspecting that the world was destined for darkness. But think about what was going on in 1809 that was not in the news at all.

In that year, Charles Darwin was born, Abraham Lincoln was born, Alfred Lord Tennyson was born as was Oliver Wendel Holmes, Cyrus McCormick, Felix Mendelssohn, Frederick Chopin, Elizabeth Barrett Browning. As bad as things looked in 1809, hope was reigning supreme. Greatness was bursting out all over, but it was not all that visible at the time for the source of that hope and greatness was lying in a crib in obscure places all across the globe.

I had my brother surf the Internet for babies born around the time of the outbreak of World War I when darkness prevailed over all of Europe. He came upon such names as Mother Teresa, Jacques Cousteau, Tennessee Williams, Ingrid Bergman, all born in 1910. Whatever might be happening in the world that might be a source of despair and dismay and disgust, whatever might be happening that might have us believe that the world is heading in a bad direction, there is always the reality of babies being born who may grow up to be just what the doctor orders to remedy a sick world. That is why it is so vital and so important that we be extra protective of babies, both born and unborn.

I am reminded here of something that occurred just a few years after Napoleon's reign. It was 1814 and Russian and Austrian armies were engaging in a little payback for what Napoleon had done to their countries. They marched through villages in Italy massacring every man, woman, and child. In one village a group of women fled with their children to a church for safety, but the soldiers followed them and slew them before the altar. One mother, however, with an infant at her breast, managed to sneak up into the balcony eluding the soldiers. The baby she was holding was none other than Giuseppe Verdi, the composer who has given us such marvelous operas as *Rigoletto*, *Il Trovatore*, and *La Traviata*, operas which are still lifting people's hearts and minds to God.

You have to wonder what other artists or composers or inventors or musicians or explorers might have had a similarly positive impact on history and on life had they as babies been as lucky as Verdi and escaped death at the hands of those Russian and Austrian armies back in 1814.

When a baby's life is taken away, be it by abortion, be it by starvation and malnutrition in some Third World country, be it by violence in some inner city alley, it is conceivable that the world might have lost someone of the magnitude of a Verdi or a Lincoln or a Schubert or a Browning. The world might have lost someone who can galvanize and unite a community like no one else can.

Somebody snatched six-month-old Denise Miller from her carriage inside a drugstore in Harlow, England, while a store clerk distracted her mother. Police found her after one of the biggest police hunts in all of British history. A team of 200 policemen and detectives had methodically questioned over 75,000 people. Three hundred twenty newspapers all across the British Isles published police questionnaires related to the kidnapping, all with the hope of finding someone who could help. Thousands upon thousands of people showered the family with letters of concern and prayer. When the baby was found and returned safely to the mom, Police Chief William Victor said: "It was like Christmas in all of England as all of the British Isles rejoiced!"

I know of a baby lost to cancer this past year. I attended a fundraiser to help defray expenses needed for a last hope effort to heal the child. I was overwhelmed not only by the immensity and expense of the donations being raffled but most especially by the scores of people who came to the event. I could not help but note how that baby touched more hearts and moved more hearts and brought more strangers together and initiated more friendships than might a whole army of people who had full lifetimes to do the same.

Recall, if you will, Baby Faye or that baby that was wedged in a shaft of an abandoned well. You might recall how those stories generated tears and cheers all across the country, not to mention the entire world. No one can bring together more people and generate more good will and compassion and generosity than can a baby, especially if that baby is in need of help.

So whether it be who they ultimately become or whether it be they themselves, babies can yield a tremendous impact upon the entire world. Roaring Camp may have been a fictional town but it well could have been a real town. When you think about it, either in an immediate way or a distant way, no man or woman can escape their influence, no man or woman can escape their impact no matter who they might happen to be.

For this whole duration of Christmas, we have been paying tribute to a young baby who seemed pretty insignificant to everyone except those shepherds and those three Wise Men who knew otherwise. The baby Jesus would prove to be the beacon of hope, the galvanizer of the human race, the breath of fresh air for which the world had desperately longed.

So on this Epiphany day, it might do us well to think about the fact that perhaps some baby born today will be the one who will come up with a drug to cure cancer or MS or Alzheimer's disease. Perhaps some baby born today will be the one to get Bosnians and Serbs, the Catholics and the Protestants in Northern Ireland, and the Arabs and Jews in the Middle East to live in peace. Perhaps some baby born today will write operas better than *Rigoletto* and *La Traviata* or write poetry better than Elizabeth Barrett Browning or will do more for the poor than Mother Teresa. Perhaps some baby born today will be the one who will come up with a way that will allow the blind to see, the deaf to hear, or the lame to walk again.

As we entertain those thoughts, it thus behooves us, on this Epiphany day, to do what we can so that no baby will miss out on life due to abortion or poverty or violence. It behooves us on this Epiphany day to do what we can to get people to come together and to open their hearts and their wallets so cures can be found and safeguards can be initiated and warnings can be acted upon so fewer and fewer will be the times when a baby in trouble or in danger initiates such action.

----

1. Bret Harte, *Luck of Roaring Camp* (New York: Dover Publications, 1992).

2. Described by John C. Maxwell, *Developing the Leader Within You* (Nashville: Thomas Nelson Publisher, 1993), p. xi.

If You Build It They Will Come

Scripture Lesson: John 13:31-33, 34-35
"... Love one another ..."

A look into the power and potential of a good example!

Besides being credited with many inventions and innovations and discoveries, Ben Franklin has also been cited for bringing light to the streets of Philadelphia. It proved to be one of his most interesting accomplishments. Initially, the city fathers were opposed to street lighting and the citizenry were not entirely thrilled with the idea. Even though Franklin strongly argued as to its benefits, it fell upon deaf ears. It was then that he embarked on an action that would bring light to every corner of every street in Philadelphia. All he did was hang a beautiful lantern on a long bracket in front of his house. Every evening he quietly cleaned the wick, polished the glass, and lit the lamp.

The light drew attention from his neighbors. It wouldn't be long before they desired one, too. The desire then spread to the adjoining neighborhoods and shortly thereafter all the streets of Philadelphia were adorned with light. Ben Franklin provided an example of the benefit of street lighting; that example became a catalyst for bringing something good into life.

There's great power in a good example. Better than any statistic, argument, or positive rationale, an example has proven to be an excellent incentive for getting done what needs to be done. They say that actions speak louder than words. I would like to amend that and say that examples speak louder than words.

When it comes to bypass surgery, doctors will tell you that nothing is more helpful in the lessening of a patient's apprehension and anxiety than the sight of someone who has successfully undergone that same operation. The surgeon can quote wonderful statistics, bring the patient all kinds of charts, or cite all the success stories in the world, but nothing can beat a visit by someone who is living proof of its positive outcome. Real life examples are not only excellent incentives for a needed action, but they're also a great means of convincing skeptics of a truth. You can say things until you're blue in the face, you can present the greatest arguments in the world, but there's nothing quite like the power of a good example.

The fiftieth anniversary of the end of World War II recalled many stories surrounding that war. There's one I recently read which speaks to the point at hand. French soldiers were walking off a ship in a British port shortly after the end of a battle they did not win. As one might expect, they were lifeless and full of despair. Their spirits were totally deflated for they knew that they had not just lost a battle, but they had lost a country.

A second ship then docked at the same port. Emerging from that ship were French soldiers called the Brigade of Guards. They emerged with their heads held high. Their uniforms looked perfect, their equipment precisely as it ought to be. On the dock, they stiffened their lips, squared their shoulders, and marched on proudly and with great vigor. The French soldiers from the first ship caught sight of the march of the Brigade and slowly in their eyes a light began to be reborn. In a matter of minutes, they too squared their shoulders, straightened out their uniforms, and marched behind the Brigade of Guards beaming with great vigor and great pride. The power of an example had changed dispirited, defeated men. It gave them back their hope and their self-respect and their pride.

An example can provide a tremendous incentive for a needed action. An example can convince a skeptic of a truth better than any statistic, any graph, or any argument. An example can uplift and inspire the most defeated and discouraged of individuals. And an example can also make possible what many thought was impossible.

Roger Bannister was the greatest proof of that. Those of you a little grayer than I will always remember that name. He became famous in 1954 for breaking a barrier that most people thought couldn't be broken. He ran the mile that year in less than four minutes, a goal that for thousands of years was deemed beyond human reach. What proved to be most interesting was what happened after he broke the barrier. Within one year of that accomplishment, 37 other runners also ran the mile in less than four minutes. And in the year after that, 300 other runners did the same. Today high school kids do it regularly.

Now, was it a case of better training, a case of better sneakers, and maybe a faster track? Not so at all. It was a case of one example providing proof that something could be done. That one example spurred countless others to stop heeding the naysayers and to pursue what was thought to be impossible to pursue.

So whether it be street lighting in Philadelphia, or patients going into surgery with a little less apprehension, whether it be pumping life into a discouraged and defeated group of soldiers, or the realization of an impossible goal, there's no substitute for an example. There's no substitute for having someone actually demonstrate what words or arguments or dreams might be trying to accomplish or say. An example is a tremendously powerful incentive and extremely effective motivator that can serve as a sedative for fear and an antidote for despair. It can make possible the impossible and it can make probable the improbable. If you're looking for the single most effective way of furthering a cause, of advancing a dream, of promoting an idea, if you're looking for the most effective means of generating enthusiasm, of initiating a mission, provide an example! You'll be surprised as to the power of its effectiveness.

I believe that Jesus knew better than anyone did the reality of that truth; he knew full well the power of example. The washing of his disciples' feet, which we commemorate on Holy Thursday, was his way of demonstrating the truth and exercising the power. Thanks to that moving and extraordinary example of humility, the apostles never got caught up in the trappings of power. They persisted to their death in humility and graciousness and service to others.

In today's Gospel, those same apostles are being urged by Jesus to love one another, for Jesus knew it would be the power of the example of that love that would be the single most effective way of winning people over to the cause for which he would die. As long as they loved one another, the Church would grow beyond limits.

There was a movie that was made several years back that has become somewhat of a classic. I'm referring to Kevin Costner's *Field of Dreams*. It's a beautiful, whimsical story about a young farmer who hears a voice in the cornfields say to him: "If you build it, he will come." "Build what?" he wants to know. He learns that he's to build a ballpark. "Who will come?" he wants to know. He learns that it would be Shoeless Joe Jackson, the great star of the Chicago White Sox.

So the farmer plows under his corn and begins to build a ball diamond. Not long afterwards, Shoeless Joe Jackson walks out of the cornfield and begins to play ball, as do seven other White Sox players and some New York Giants and also the farmer's father who had some unfinished business to attend to with his son. Eventually you see all sorts of cars from every corner of the United States coming to the ballpark to see them play.

It's a warm and tender story. It probably sounds crazy if you haven't seen it. But if you think about it, it captures in a metaphorical way the point Jesus was trying to make with his disciples. He was telling them that if they build a Church where love is practiced, where love is evident, where examples of love are plentiful, they will come. People will come; people will join; people will flock there. Not because of what is preached or being said or being promoted, but because of what they see in the flesh among its members. They will come because of the lanterns of love hung by communities of Christians noted and distinguished because they did indeed love each other.

When Red Jacket, the great orator of the Seneca Indians, was urged to become a Christian, he told the missionaries that the Christians must first prove their faith. "Go then," he said, "and show me Christianity in action. Select, for example, the people of Buffalo and have them display your faith. We will be silent and remain spectators. Get them to improve their morals and refine their habits. Make them less disposed to cheat the Indians, to make them drunk, or to take them from their lands. Let us know the tree by the blossoms and the blossoms by the fruit. When this shall be made clear to our minds we'll be more willing to listen to you and come over to Christ but, until then, we must be allowed to follow the religion of our ancestors."

Red Jacket was in essence telling those missionaries: "If you build it, we will come." But since they didn't or couldn't build it, neither he nor his Indian brothers or sisters were willing to come.

Perhaps that sums up the reason why Christianity never did realize its potential. The early disciples did a good job of heeding Christ's words; they did create caring communities where examples of love were in evidence. They behaved, so to speak, like the French Brigade of Guards and people lined up to march right behind them. As time advanced, however, so did the examples diminish. The more they diminished the lesser the attraction and less was the willingness of outsiders to embark on and heed the call to Christ.

An American teacher was employed in Japan with the understanding that, during school hours, he would not utter a word on the subject of Christianity. He kept his part of the bargain. He lived before his students the Christ's life but he never spoke of it to them; not a word was said to influence the young men and women committed to his care. But so beautiful was his character, so blameless was the example of his life that forty of his students, unbeknownst to him, met in a grove and signed a secret covenant to abandon idolatry. Twenty-five of them sought formal training in the Christian faith and several went into the ministry.

That American teacher provided an example, that was all. He didn't preach to them, didn't cajole them, didn't show graphs or statistics, didn't present arguments as to the benefits and the beauty of the Christian faith. He merely hung the lantern of his life in the middle of that classroom. His life's example took on the dimensions of that stadium in that cornfield: he built it, and they came.

That's our challenge today. That's our call. There are people out there starving for the message of Jesus. There are people out there who are willing to come over to our faith, but we have to build something for them to come to. That building is the example of a life of love.

My friends, heed the suggestion of Red Jacket and start showing the blossoms and the fruits of your faith. Show with your lives the care and concern that marked the life of Jesus. Hang a lantern in the corner of your street, a lantern like the one the American teacher hung in his classroom. Be the Brigade of Guards for the discouraged and the dispirited with whom you live and whom you know. Be the evidence of truth for those unconvinced of the veracity of claims and statistics. Be a Roger Bannister and set off a tidal wave of other examples of the faith. Do that! Build that! Believe me! They will come!

Catfish

Scripture Lesson: Romans 8:1-5
... we even boast of our afflictions ...

We may not appreciate problems or difficulties but they can work a blessing.

In the days of old, fishermen who sailed the seas had wells sunk into the bottoms of their boats. When they caught or netted fish, they placed them in those wells where they stayed alive until the boat reached the shore. One of the problems encountered by those fishermen was that the fish in those wells would lose their vigor and vitality. The cramped environment took "the wind out of their gills" and when they'd be emptied into bins for sale to the fish dealers, they didn't appear freshly caught and the consumer would complain as to their taste and their flavor.

That was true of all the fishing boats and all the fishermen save one. That one brought fish to shore that looked as though they'd just been caught. Fish dealers literally fought for the right to buy his fish. Not only did they look the freshest but consumers claimed they were the best when it came to flavor. His fellow fishermen held the man in awe. They longed to learn how he could deliver fish that appeared so much fresher and healthier than their own. The matter remained a mystery until the day of the old fisherman's death when, according to her father's instructions, his daughter revealed the secret.

Her father, she said, kept a ferocious catfish in the well of his boat. Although that catfish would eat a few of the fish, it kept the other fish moving, stirring, and on the alert, fighting for their very lives. When those fish were emptied into the bins of those dealers on shore, they looked fresh and healthy and as if they'd just been hooked out of the deep blue sea.

Lest we think that fisherman cruel for inserting an ugly and hostile catfish in the well of his ship, consider the fact that it ensured that the highest quality of fish would make it to the marketplace. Although those fish may not have appreciated the fight for their lives, it made them the most popular of all the fish caught that day.

I tell you that fish story because I believe there is a lot of similarity between that story and life. Many people have risen to extraordinary heights, many have excelled in life, many have won great admiration, many have become human beings of the highest possible quality and caliber thanks, in no small measure, to a catfish that got dropped into the well of their life.

I read an article on depression that named child prodigies as the group most highly susceptible to depression once they reach adulthood. In their analysis, the authors of the article pointed to the fact that those children were not used to failure, or trauma, or difficulty. Their amazing skills and talents came their way naturally with little or no struggle on their part, and their application of those skills and talents resulted in their experiencing one success after another. Their childhood was virtually free of any experience that hinted of adversity and, being special, they were often treated as celebrities. They were treated "with kid gloves."

So when these child prodigies made their way into adulthood and began experiencing the usual problems that accompany that move, they had no coping skills, they had no experience at dealing with adversity. Simple problems proved overwhelming and minor difficulties proved monumental. That would result in bout after bout of depression.

As a general rule, most children share the well of their life with a catfish, which means that hardly a day will go by when they won't stub their toe or find a toy broken or get swatted by a playmate or meet up with failure or meet with the realization that they can't always get their way. The plus side of the catfish, the good of the adversity, is that it will promote maturity, it will hone coping skills and will, most especially and importantly, make him or her an adult able and ready to face the abundance of difficulties and problems associated with adulthood. They will be more resistant to the depression that afflicts child prodigies whose childhood was no way near as difficult as theirs.

Catfish in our wells do an excellent job of preparing us for life's inevitable shortcomings and disasters. Besides that, they also help breed compassion.

One day, an eight-year-old boy and his dad entered a pet store in search of a puppy. As they looked over a litter of newborns, the boy couldn't help but notice one puppy with a limp. Inquiring as to the limp, he was told by the store manager that the puppy was born with a bad leg and nothing could be done to fix it. The boy quickly turned to his dad and, after a short conversation, the dad told the manager that he wished to purchase the puppy with the limp. The manager, a bit dumbfounded, said: "You know this dog is never going to run and jump and play with your son. How about I sell you one of the healthier ones?" Upon hearing that, the boy reached down and rolled up one side of his pants revealing a badly crippled leg supported by a metal brace. He looked up at the manager and said: "Look, Mister, I don't run or jump well myself. The little puppy with the limp is the one I want. I understand what he is going through, and he's going to need someone who understands."

A catfish in the well of our life is a great provider of compassion and understanding. Having a taste of the pain and suffering and trials common to life means we are less likely to be as self-righteous, as callous, as judgmental, or as apathetic as might be the case with those who have never known adversity, those who never had a catfish fall into the well of their life.

It reminds me of a *Peanuts* cartoon that happened to appear on Thanksgiving Day. Linus asked Charlie Brown if he was going to have a big meal. Charlie says: "I guess so, but I don't think much about food!" Then Snoopy lets out this huff. Looking at his empty dish, he says to himself: "Charlie would think a lot about food if his dish were as empty as mine!" Catfish do a great job of acquainting us with adversity, of acquainting us with the kind of hardships that some people go through in spades.

The third thing that catfish can do is to call out from us talent and ability, which may have never been uncovered had adversity not come our way. Oliver Goldsmith had his heart set on being a doctor but his application to medical school was met with rejection. He was bitterly disappointed but in his disappointment he turned to writing. Eight years later, *The Vicar of Wakefield*,[1] one of literature's great classics, was given to the world. Nathaniel Hawthorne and Charles Dickens had a similar experience. Dickens had his heart set on being an actor while Hawthorne wished to be a customs official. Neither one could realize his dream; in their disappointment, they turned to writing. Three of history's greatest writers may never have practiced their craft had a catfish called disappointment not been dropped into the wells of their lives.

Catfish can help us prepare for life's inevitable shortcomings. They can help us be more compassionate. They can help us unearth talent and ability we may never have known we had. Fourthly, they can be great teachers.

When Ben Franklin was seven years old he made a mistake which he remembered for seventy years. When he was a lad of seven, he fell in love with a whistle. He was so excited about it that he went to the toy shop, piled his money on the counter, and demanded the whistle, not caring or thinking at all of the price.

"I then came home," he wrote to a friend seventy years later, "and went whistling all over the house, much pleased with my whistle. But then I got scolded for making all kinds of noise and, when they learned what I had paid for the whistle, they laughed and laughed because I had paid ten times what it was actually worth. The tears and the embarrassment which that provided me," wrote Franklin, "helped teach me a lesson that stayed with me my entire life."

From that day forward, Ben Franklin became very vigilant. He would always make sure that something was of value before he would ever invest the time, the energy, and the money which that something may have required. The catfish that entered Ben Franklin's well at the age of seven proved to be an invaluable teacher.

That holds true as well for other catfish that enter life's well. The irritation, the adversity, the embarrassment, the pain they may cause can help steer a life away from the pitfalls and traps common to the more naive and less enlightened among us.

I am reminded of one of the theories as to why Jimmy Carter failed as a president. The fault, it was claimed, rested with his advisors. It was theorized that they were too young and too inexperienced. Had they been older and thus more familiar with the disappointments, the problems, and the difficulties common to the Washington scene, Jimmy Carter might not have been led into the kind of mistakes which resulted in his downfall as president. A catfish in our well provides us with experience in dealing with adversity, experience that provides invaluable lessons as to what we should or should not do when it comes to our carving a successful path through life.

Catfish can help us prepare for life's inevitable shortcomings, they can help us be more compassionate, they can help us unearth talent we never knew we had, they can be great teachers, and lastly they can be the stimulant for a great life.

A colleague took his son to see the Great Barrier Reef that stretches 1,800 miles from New Guinea to Australia. He noted that the coral polyps on the reef facing the quiet and tranquil lagoon appeared pale and lifeless. The coral facing the pounding waves and surging tides of the open sea were bright and vibrant with splendid colors and very flowery growth. Asking a guide the reason for the difference, my colleague was told that it was very simple. The coral on the lagoon side gets no stimulation so its growth is very stunted. The coral facing the surging power of the open sea thrives and multiplies because it is challenged and tested and stimulated by the pounding of the waves.

What holds true for coral holds true for us. The catfish in the well of a life, the failure and trouble that life can deliver, will often stimulate us and challenge us and push us to heights we may never have reached had the water in our wells not had a catfish to stir things up. Consider, if you will, the best teachers we ever had. They probably weren't very popular during our tenure at school precisely because of their catfish qualities. But thanks to those qualities, we put our nose to the grindstone and learned our lessons and we're the better for it today.

Saint Paul, in our second reading, talks about how people of faith boast of their afflictions. They boast of their afflictions because the overwhelming majority saw those afflictions as doing to them what the catfish did to those fish in the well of the old fisherman's boat. It made them people of the highest possible quality and caliber.

My friends, if a catfish falls into the well of your life, consider it a blessing. Unlike the child prodigy, you will be less prone to depression. Like the boy and that puppy, you will be better able to understand and sympathize with those who are hurting. Like Dickens and Hawthorne and Goldsmith, you may find a talent that you might not have otherwise discovered. Like Ben Franklin, you will know better the next time you are tempted to invest in something that isn't worth the investment. Like the coral on the ocean side of the Great Barrier Reef, you will be more vibrant, more alive, and more colorful. My friends, you may never have thought of boasting of your afflictions, but maybe you should. Maybe after leaving aside the pain or the indignity they may have caused you, you'll find that they've done you well!

---

1. Oliver Goldsmith, *The Vicar of Wakefield* (New York: Penguin Books, 1982).

The Critic's Choice

Scripture Lesson: Exodus 16:2-4, 12-15
"I have heard the grumbling of the Israelites ..."

Some thoughts to ponder should complaints or criticism come your way.

The humorous story is told of an Italian monk who went to the monastery at Montserrat, Spain. One of the requirements at Montserrat was perpetual silence. The monks were only allowed to speak after two years and then they were permitted to say only two words. After two more years went by, they were allowed to say two more words and so on: two years, two words. When the first two years had passed, the new monk was called before his superior to make his first two-word statement. The monk's first two words were: "Bed hard." Two more years passed and his next set of two words was: "Food bad." After another two years went by, the monk appeared before his superior and said: "I quit." The superior looked at him and replied: "That doesn't surprise me at all. All you've done since you've been here is complain and criticize."

I mention that humorous story because I want to talk with you today about complaining and criticizing. Rare is the life that has not been on its receiving end, and more than a few could honestly say that they can't remember when there wasn't someone complaining about or criticizing what they happen to be doing. That being so, I thought I would offer you some thoughts to ponder should complaints and criticism come your way.

First of all, you have to understand that it comes with the territory called life. Every role we assume in life will find us experiencing criticism and hearing complaints. Let's take for starters the role of a parent. The most difficult lesson for every parent to learn is that parenting is not a popularity contest. Criticism from one's child is inevitable if you're going to be a parent.

A friend of mine told me that when children enter into adolescence, between the years twelve to seventeen, it's like they go into a cave. He described it as the cave years. They go down into this cave away from their parents because they've come to believe that their parents can't do anything right. He said that the only way to handle them is to throw a little meat into the cave and close the door.

I love the advertisement that went: "A set of encyclopedias for sale. Never used. Teenage son knows everything." I believe that every parent has to understand that the teenage years are often the years when the child is dealing with a lot of changes. Part of those changes involve rebellion, and rebellion translates into criticism. The parent needs to roll with the punches as the teenager needs to roll with the changes.

No matter what position or role you hold in life, be it parent or doctor or nurse or whatever, you're going to find a lot of people behaving like teenagers. A lot will give you the impression that you can't do anything right. What you have to realize is that complaining and criticism come with the territory that we call life.

The second thing you need to realize is that there are an awful lot of people who love to criticize, who love to call attention to imperfections.

I read recently of something John Keats, the famous poet, once did. He wrote a poem in which he referenced Cortez and not Balboa as the discoverer of the Pacific Ocean. There were three schools of thought as to why he did it. The first was that Keats did not know that Cortez did not discover the Pacific Ocean. The second asserted that he wrote Cortez because he needed a two-syllable word instead of three. The third maintained, and it proved to be true, that Keats wanted to know if anyone read his poetry. He believed that if they did, he'd be barraged with all kinds of letters telling him what an ignoramus he was not to know that Balboa and not Cortez discovered the Pacific Ocean. Many letters did indeed come and so Keats knew that people read his poetry.

There are an awful lot of people who have seemed to make it their life's work to notice and see and call attention to every little thing that might not be perfect. They seem to get a lot of satisfaction out of letting us know when we made a mistake or when we didn't do something the way it's supposed to be done. They seem to have forgotten, or they don't wish to face, the reality that perfection is something reserved for God.

So first, complaining and criticizing comes with the territory called life. Second, complaining and criticizing springs eternal from those who can't reconcile the fact that we live in an imperfect world. And third, complaining and criticizing have followed the work of some of the greatest achievers in all of history.

Two of history's greatest poets — Walt Whitman and Robert Frost — were both criticized for what they wrote. One reviewer of *The London Critic* stated confidently: "Whitman is as adequate with the art of poetry as a hog is with mathematics." The poetry editor of *The Atlantic Monthly* told a 28-year-old Frost that his magazine had no room for poor poets. In 1889 Rudyard Kipling received the following letter from *The San Francisco Examiner*: "I'm sorry, Mr. Kipling, but you just don't know how to use the English language." At age seventeen, Wayne Gretzky was told by someone in authority that he would not be able to survive in a hockey rink.

Eric Segal wrote the book called *Love Story*[1]. The book was made into a movie. Almost with a single voice, the critics condemned both the movie and the novel. The book was one of the largest selling books ever written and the movie was a box office smash. Albert Einstein once stated: "The great spirits have always encountered violent opposition from mediocre minds."

As much as critics and complainers have much to tell us about the things that we create and the work that we do, they are not the last word and they are not the only word. As evidenced by Whitman and Frost and Kipling and Gretzky, they're often far from right when it comes to the assessment of talent. You can rest assured that no matter how great are the things that we do, a good number of complaints and criticism will inevitably follow.

The fourth thing to consider when complaints and criticism come our way is that we're often absorbing what is really not meant for us. Years ago, Hall of Fame coach Don Shula was vacationing in Maine with his wife and five children. On a rainy afternoon they went into the town's only theater. Walking in, they encountered only six people, every one of whom stood up to applaud the Shulas. Don and his family sat down and a man ran up and shook Don's hand. "How did you recognize me?" Don asked. "Mister," the man said, "I don't know who you are. All I know is that, just before your family walked in, the manager said that unless five more people show up we weren't going to see the movie."

Just as that applause was not meant for Don Shula personally, so can complaints and criticisms be not meant for us personally. There are people always angry and critical at the male species in general. There are people always angry and critical at the female species in general. There are people angry and critical at priests in general. There are people angry and critical at doctors in general. It could well be that, when you're getting an earful of criticism, it's not you personally whom they're critical of, it's whom or what you happen to represent.

I sat on the Board of Directors of the Credit Union of Sisters Hospital for many years. Anyone who is familiar with credit unions knows that each year an examiner comes and goes over the books and operation to make sure that everything is on the up-and-up. We had an examiner one year who was unbelievably critical of everything we did. It looked as though we could do nothing right. We sat there and he lambasted us for many of our actions and procedures. We knew that we ran a good ship and so we couldn't believe the kind of hammering we were receiving.

That examiner never did finish the report. He was replaced two weeks later and we were told that he would not be coming back. He had been admitted to Buffalo General Hospital's Hospice Unit. What we hadn't known was that the man was a cancer patient trying to hold onto his job as long as he could. The criticism and the lambasting that we received were not really directed at us as a credit union; it was merely a by-product of the misery and pain and suffering that he had been experiencing with his cancer. Critics and complainers are often venting their own personal anguish. As much as they might be dumping on us, it's not us that's the problem — it's them.

76

The fifth thing to consider should complaints and criticisms come our way is that no statue was ever erected to honor a critic. Statues are for the criticized.

The most noble and notable of human beings, one of the great humanitarians of all time, was Dr. Albert Schweitzer. Shortly after he arrived in Africa, where he began to build hospitals and care for the sick, he was told by a colleague that there were people back in his hometown who wished to convey some criticism about the way he was proceeding. Dr. Schweitzer had a great retort. He said to his colleague: "You tell my critics that I like my way of doing things better than their way of not doing things."

It always seems to be true that those who do the biggest amount of complaining and criticizing are usually those sitting on their duffs while everyone else is giving of his or her time and talents. And there are always those who out of jealousy complain and criticize in the hopes that their remarks will take some shine off the fine and wonderful work of a colleague whose popularity they resent.

The sixth and last thing to consider when complaints and criticisms come our way is that maybe we deserve it and maybe we ought to pay attention to what's being said. Dr. Norman Vincent Peale once wrote: "The trouble with most of us is that we would rather be ruined by praise than saved by criticism." How true that is and how often has it happened when we figured that our friends were the ones who were right and our critics were the ones who were wrong. We didn't want to admit that our friends were telling us what we wanted to hear while our critics were telling us what we needed to hear. We just couldn't face that truth.

Moses, in our first reading, is on the receiving end of a tremendous amount of complaining and criticizing. Despite his leading them out of slavery, people were finding fault with his actions. It seemed he was doing nothing right. Jesus would undergo a similar experience with those whom he specifically came to save. They did nothing but bombard him with complaints and criticisms, directing more than a few towards the good things he was doing.

The next time you're hit with complaints and criticisms, first remember that you're not only rubbing shoulders with Frost and

Walt Whitman but you are also rubbing shoulders with Moses and you're even rubbing shoulders with Jesus. Second, remember that it comes with the territory called life. Third, remember that there are a lot of people who love to pick on our imperfections. Fourth, remember it could be that you're not the target. Fifth, remember they've never built a statue to a critic. Sixth, remember what you're hearing could very well be a truth your loved ones were reluctant to tell. And lastly, be grateful that you're on the receiving end and not the giving end of complaints and criticism. It's a much greater and far more honorable and a far more prestigious place to be.

---

1. Eric Segal, *Love Story* (New York: Harper & Row, 1970).

Asking

Scripture Lesson: Matthew 4:12-23
"Come after me and I will make you fishers of men."

A look at why it's important to ask.

———————————

The late Speaker of the House Thomas "Tip" O'Neill once told of a valuable lesson he learned early in his career. In 1935, during his very first political campaign, a neighbor told him: "I am going to vote for you tomorrow even though you didn't ask me to!" A shocked O'Neill replied: "Why, Mrs. O'Brien, I have lived across from you for eighteen years, I cut your grass in the summer, I shoveled your walk in the winter, I didn't think I had to ask for your vote." Mrs. O'Brien replied: "Tom, let me tell you something: people like to be asked!"

I found that out for myself just a few short months ago. I had attended the death of a patient here at Sisters Hospital, and the family asked that I preside at the funeral. The patient belonged to St. Ambrose Parish where I had been the associate pastor for some seven years and where I still help out on various occasions. The pastor is one of my closest friends. So I told the family that I'd take care of the arrangements with the church. I merely called St. Ambrose and told the secretary to tell the pastor that I would be presiding at the funeral.

When I arrived that morning at the church, the pastor was there to help me set up. He said to me: "You know I don't care about your taking a funeral here at any time. You can do anything you want in this parish, but it would be nice that instead of telling me, you asked me." I discovered then and there that Mrs. O'Brien was indeed right: people like to be asked.

When you give it a thought, there's much truth in that statement. Being asked is often heartwarming and often very uplifting. It's a sign of respect as well as one of courtesy. In many cases, being asked means being affirmed and recognized as someone of value and worth.

In my work as a priest, I have occasion to talk with people who have lost a husband or wife. They often tell me that one of the things that hurts the most is the fact that many of the couples, with whom they once associated, don't ask them out anymore. Maybe it's because they feel awkward asking or maybe they feel he or she will feel awkward being asked. But the fact is that by not asking they are sending a message that he or she doesn't belong, that he or she is someone no one wants to associate with anymore.

The elderly often experience much the same problem. As they get older, fewer people ask them to do things. Many times it's because people honestly feel that it might be too much for them, it might be more than they can handle, an honest concern. Unfortunately, however, not being asked sends a message that they are not needed anymore, not important anymore, not useful anymore.

Interestingly enough, a similar case can be made for the very young. One of my favorite stories concerns a grandmother, a mother, and a little boy who walked into a restaurant and sat down to order. The waitress took the grandmother's order, then the mother's order, and then she turned to the little boy and asked: "What would you like?" The mother immediately said: "Oh, I will order for him." The waitress, without being overly rude, ignored the mother and again asked the little boy: "What would you like?" The mother once again spoke up: "I will order for him!" The waitress ignored her yet again and asked the little boy one more time: "What would you like?" "I would like a hamburger!" he stammered. "How would you like your hamburger?" asked the waitress. "Would you like it with onion, mustard, and the works?" His mouth now open in amazement, the boy said: "Yes, I would like the works!" The waitress went over to the window and she howled the grandmother's order, then the mother's order, and then in a loud voice she said: "And a hamburger with the works!" The little boy turned to his mother in utter astonishment and said: "Gee, Mommy! She thinks I am real!" That waitress, by asking the little boy what he wanted, provided him with status. The asking gave him recognition; it gave him a feeling of importance that he had never had before.

So whether it be a widow or widower, an elderly man or woman, a little boy or a little girl, they all bear out the truth of Mrs. O'Brien's remark to Tip O'Neill: "People like to be asked!" And, in their case, the asking is a matter of letting them know that they are not out of the mainstream of life, that they are not useless or irrelevant or unimportant. Asking them out, asking them to do something, personally asking them what their desires may be, carries significance often overlooked.

Then there's the matter of opening up doors to experiences of great enrichment, opening up doors of opportunity for excitement and satisfaction and fulfillment. Asking can do that as well.

I remember, when I was eighteen years old, my optometrist, Dr. Steven Gladysz (whose office was right next door to my father's store), asked me to coach the Assumption School baseball team. They needed a coach and he asked me if I'd take the job. I don't know what possessed me to say yes but I did. That began for me a fourteen-year odyssey as a baseball coach that sometimes involved the handling of four teams a season. I could talk until next year about some of the wonderful experiences I have had, the extraordinary people I have met. I presided over the marriages of a good many of the kids I coached. I baptized their babies and claim many of them as good friends.

As a result of coaching, my life has been enriched beyond measure and that wouldn't have been the case had my optometrist, Dr. Steven Gladysz, not asked me to coach the Assumption team. Looking back, had it not been advertised in the church bulletin that they needed a coach, I would not have volunteered. If I were told they were looking for a coach, I would not have volunteered. But because I was asked, I did. The asking opened for me a door to an experience of great enrichment, which I would have otherwise missed had I not been asked.

Many of you, I believe, can speak of similar experiences. I'm sure many of you can tell of how someone asked you to do something and how that something did for you and your life what baseball did for mine. That is why I often encourage people to ask others to help them or to ask others to participate in some cause because the asking could do for them what Dr. Steven Gladysz' asking did for me.

The Diocese of Buffalo, for the past several years, has implemented a program which is titled "Called by Name." It is a vocation recruitment program where men and women, priests and parishes send in names of those who they feel might make good priests or religious. Those named are asked to attend a meeting where they'd be introduced to the world of priesthood and religious life with the hope that they might give it some consideration. The program began because vocation directors came to discover that one of the reasons why many a man or woman never gave the priesthood or religious life a thought was because no one asked them to give it a thought. I'm embarrassed to say that I never asked anyone to give it a thought and I wonder if, by not asking, I might have kept someone from opening a door to a life that has been for me one of tremendous enrichment and fulfillment and satisfaction.

In the Gospel today, Peter, James, and John were asked by Jesus to take on the work of discipleship. That asking gave the three of them a life that they would have never realized or experienced had they not been asked. It opened for them a door to an unbelievable adventure they would never regret. As Mrs. O'Brien pointed out to Tip O'Neill, people like to be asked. That's not only because it gives the sense that they're important and needed and wanted but also because it gets them to consider an option which would otherwise not be considered, an option that could open for them a door to experiences they will cherish and love and never regret.

Then there's the matter of asking being a means of lessening the sting of a pain or hurt or tragedy. In a book, *The Facts of Death*[1], Michael A. Simpson describes the "horse on a dining room table" syndrome. "At a dinner party," says Simpson, "a horse is sitting in the middle of the table but we all talk as if the horse weren't there. We fear the host will be embarrassed if it's mentioned at all. The host, in turn, doesn't refer to the horse lest it upset us!" Though it is ignored in conversation, the horse sits there as big as life in the middle of the table as well as in the center of our thoughts and minds during the duration of the dinner party.

You find that often occurring in places of work when someone who has lost a loved one returns to the job a few days after the funeral. No one asks them about the death. No one asks if they miss the one they lost. No one asks them anything pertaining to what is probably the worst thing that ever happened to them in their life. Those people would like to talk about the horse that's on the table. They'd like to vent some of the pain they are feeling. They'd like to know that there are people who care about how much they are hurting. But if no one asks, everything is left in the air, everything is kept inside, and everyone goes about his or her business doing one's darndest to avoid any mention of the horse that is sitting in the middle of the dining room table.

A somewhat similar thread runs through another common occurrence. John Powell, the Jesuit author, writes about it in a recent book[2]. He was presiding at Mass and when it came time for communion, he passed by a little boy who wasn't old enough to receive the Lord in the Eucharist. At the end of Mass, he happened to notice that the little boy had his lip protruding just a bit. Being asked by Powell if anything was wrong, the boy, after an initial denial, burst into tears and blurted out: "You passed me by at communion time because you don't like me!" John Powell was quick to assure him that he had it all wrong, that he liked him very much. He went on to explain to the boy that he first had to make his First Communion before he could receive the Lord in the Eucharist.

The whole event made Powell wonder about the damage he might have inflicted or the hurt that might have lingered had he not asked the boy if anything was wrong. How often has it happened that a parent, child, husband, or wife felt slighted or bruised by something that was said or done and, because no one asked if anything was wrong, the pain and hurt lingered and festered and stewed. This horse was sitting on the dining room table and they would have longed to talk about that horse but no one bothered to ask.

My friends, what Mrs. O'Brien said to Tip O'Neill was true — people like to be asked. So make it a point to do more asking. Do it out of courtesy. Don't be as presumptuous as was Tip O'Neill with Mrs. O'Brien or myself with the pastor of St. Ambrose. Do it so that widows and widowers, so that elderly men and women, so that young boys or young girls might feel they are wanted and needed and that they matter. Do more asking so that like Peter, James, and John in today's Gospel or like me and baseball, people might be afforded the opportunity to do something they might have otherwise never done had they not been asked, something that will open for them a door to an adventure of unbelievable magnitude and satisfaction and fulfillment. Do more asking so that people won't have to keep quiet about the horse on the dining room table, the horse that's breaking their heart. Do more asking so that some little boy, little girl or men or women might be provided a voice for a slight or misunderstanding that might have otherwise festered inside. As Mrs. O'Brien told Tip O'Neill: People like to be asked! — Don't forget that.

---

1. Michael A. Simpson, *The Facts of Death: A Complete Guide for Being Prepared* (Englewood Cliffs, N.J.: Prentice Hall, 1979).

2. John Powell S.J., *Solving the Riddle of Self* (Allen, Texas: Thomas More Publishing, 1995).

It's Not Fair

Scripture Lesson: Matthew 20:1-16
*"... you have put them on the same basis
as us who have worked a full day ..."*

Some things to consider when we're tempted to cry "unfair!"

If I were to catalog the most frequent expressions mouthed by hospital patients, at the top or near the top would be the expression: "It's not fair!" "Father, I exercised, I watched my diet, I did what I was supposed to do, and here I am with a heart attack. It's not fair!" "Father, he just retired, he finally had a chance to do all the things he wanted to do and now he's had a stroke and will probably never leave this bed. It's not fair!"

I'm afraid that in the world called the hospital you're going to hear very often the expression: "It's not fair!" And, if truth be told, you'll hear that same expression with just as much frequency and just as much intensity outside the world of the hospital. Unfairness is something built into life. As much as it galls us and upsets us there's no getting around the fact of its presence.

Since our Gospel parable today deals with the unfairness issue (after all, why should someone who worked one hour get paid the same as the one who worked eight), I thought that I would talk with you today about what needs to be considered whenever we utter the words, "It's not fair!"

First of all, we have to consider whether we've been fair. I love the story of the baker who suspects that the farmer who was supplying him butter was being unfair because the butter he received was never at the weight it was supposed to be. It always seemed to be a few ounces light. He carefully checked the weight and his suspicions were confirmed. So he took the farmer to court. At the trial, an embarrassing truth came out. The farmer, when called upon to explain himself, simply said that he had no scale except the old-fashioned kind where you balance one side with the other to get an even weight. He couldn't understand how the butter weight could be wrong when he used for the balance a one pound loaf of bread bought daily from the baker.

How often have we cried, "It's not fair!" when the truth is that we haven't been fair, when the truth is that our record isn't very clean when it comes to fairness? And how about the fact that we never say, "It isn't fair!" when we've been on the receiving end of a break we didn't deserve?

I remember protesting a ticket I received for speeding. I told the judge that it wasn't fair that I received the ticket when I was the slowest moving vehicle on that road the night that the officer stopped me. But you know what? There were times when I was the fastest moving vehicle on the road and I never got a ticket and I never thought that was unfair.

I'm reminded of those who have raised their voices in protest over affirmative action, who claim it's not fair that certain people get an advantage when it comes to employment opportunities. Those very same people didn't say much of anything years earlier when the unfairness affected those who are now the recipients of affirmative action.

No matter what it is, no matter who we are, we're quite vociferous when what is seen as unfair is something which happens to affect our lives, but on the other hand we're not very vocal when what we see as unfair is something that doesn't affect our life. We never shout, "It's not fair!" when we're on the receiving end of a break we didn't deserve but we'll most definitely shout "unfair" when someone other than ourselves is on the receiving end of something he or she didn't deserve.

The third thing we need to consider when we say, "It's not fair," is whether or not we're in possession of all the facts. An old woman was living in Scotland in the most abject of poverty. She never had the advantage of education and never left the borders of Scotland. She had a son who became a sailor and was then traveling the seas working for the U.S. Government. The rumors spread around the Scottish village that he had made out quite well as a sailor, that he was in fact quite prosperous. So the neighbors talked all the time about how unfair it was that this no good son was living in luxury while his mother lived in poverty.

One day, one of them ventured to ask the old lady about that son of hers and his terribly unfair negligence. "Doesn't your son ever send you any money to help you out?" asked the neighbor. "No!" said the mother but, eager to defend him, she added, "But he does write me every month telling me about the United States and how wonderful it is, and along with every letter he sends me pretty pictures." "May I see those pictures?" asked the curious neighbor. "Why, certainly you may see them. I'm proud to show them to you." She reaches up to her Bible and she shows the pictures, about thirty of them, and do you know what they were? They were bank notes which, if she knew they were money and cashed them, she'd be out of poverty and well into luxury.

How often have we judged people to be unfair? How often have we yelled, "It's not fair!" on the heels of a story, only to discover later that we had it all wrong; all the facts were not in order. What we considered to be unfair, was not unfair at all.

The fourth thing to consider when we say, "It isn't fair!" is that perhaps we're looking at fairness from only one side of a ledger. Henry David Thoreau, the famous writer of the nineteenth century, once went to jail rather than pay his poll tax to a state which supported slavery. During this period, he wrote the essay "Civil Disobedience" now famous the world over. Thoreau's good friend Ralph Waldo Emerson shared Thoreau's abhorrence to slavery but paid his poll tax. Upon hearing what happened to Thoreau, he hurried to the jail. Peering through the bars he said: "Why, Henry, what are you doing in there?" And the unbowed Thoreau replied: "No, Ralph, the question is: What are you doing out there?"

That haunting question from Thoreau, I believe, accounts for our looking at fairness from one side of the ledger, our looking at it from the receiving side and not the giving side. You'll seldom hear anyone say (and they should say) that "it's not fair" that Mother Teresa had to work so hard, or that so-and-so has to carry a burden all by himself. You seldom hear anyone say (and they should say) "it's not fair" that only a handful of people are working on a problem that's a disgrace and a disaster. My suspicion is you don't hear anyone say it because they realize that a Thoreau-type response would be in order and they'd be embarrassed into rolling up their sleeves and lending a needed hand.

The fifth thing to consider when we say, "It's not fair," is that quite often what we're complaining about, in the big picture, is hardly a matter worthy of complaint. I like the story of the poor farmer who goes to his rabbi complaining of his miserable existence living in a tiny house with his wife and two children. He tells the rabbi: "I'm so unhappy. What can I do?" And the rabbi says: "Do you have a goat outside?" The man says: "Yes!" "So then bring the goat inside the house." The next week the man returns to the rabbi: "Rabbi, it's terrible! That stinky goat has made our home even more crowded. What should I do?" The rabbi says: "Bring in the cow." The farmer comes back a week later almost at the breaking point. This time the rabbi tells the poor man: "Bring in the chickens!" When the man complains the week later, the rabbi advises him to bring in the rabbit and the following week the horse. The man finally cries: "I can't take it anymore! What shall I do?" And the rabbi advises: "Get rid of the horse, the following week the rabbit, then the chickens, then the goat, then the cow." So after doing all that, the poor man comes to the rabbi now filled with great elation. "Thank you so much, Rabbi. We're all very, very happy now and our house has all kinds of room."

So often when we complain, "It's not fair," we're complaining about something that pales by comparison to what some people accept and handle with never a word of complaint. Many times when we cry, "It's not fair," we fail to realize that outside of that minor unfairness we really have much to be grateful for and the unfairness could be far worse and a lot graver than it happens to be.

The sixth thing to consider when we say, "It's not fair," is that what's unfair could be used to work a blessing. Milo C. Jones operated a small farm in Wisconsin, barely subsisting, when disaster struck. He suffered a paralyzing stroke. His relatives were so convinced that he was a hopeless invalid that they found him a comfortable bed and merely did things to keep him comfortable. Milo Jones, however, did not see things that way. Unable to use his body, Jones turned to his mind and almost immediately he had an idea that was destined to compensate him for his misfortune. He summoned his relatives together and charged them with planting his entire acreage with corn. That corn would be used to feed a herd of pigs and those pigs would be slaughtered and turned into sausage. Within a few years, Milo C. Jones' Sausage was sold in stores across the nation; it's second only to Bob Evans in popularity and sales. An unfair happening in the life of Milo Jones could have been the worst thing in the world but he was able to work it into a blessing.

History is filled with the names of people who took advantage of an unfairness that could have diminished their life and made it into something that enhanced their life. There is not much we can do about the unfairness in life but there's a lot we can do *with* the unfairness in life.

One final point to consider when we say, "It's not fair," is that no matter how unfair things may be, there are things that are certain: God's presence, God's generosity, and God's faithful support.

I'm reminded of the pastor who was visiting a farmer who was a member of his congregation. In the course of his visit, the pastor noticed a windmill with an inscription at its base. The words were weathered and barely legible. Reading carefully, he made out the words: "God is faithful." The pastor turned to the farmer: "Do you mean that God's faithfulness depends on the direction the wind is blowing?" "Oh, no," said the farmer, "that's not it at all. It means that, regardless of which way the wind blows, God is faithful." No matter how unfair life can be, we can be certain that God will be faithful with his love, care, and support.

Today's Gospel parable always elicits cries of unfairness, not only from the protagonists within the parable but also from us who hear it. It isn't fair that people who work a measly hour get paid as much as the people who kill themselves for eight. Now maybe, just maybe, Jesus used the parable to get people to think about unfairness in different ways. Maybe he wanted those who decry unfairness to think about how they're not above being unfair themselves. Maybe he wanted those who decry unfairness to consider their silence when they are on the receiving end of a break they didn't deserve. Maybe he wanted them to check on the facts before they accuse someone of being unfair. Maybe Jesus wanted those who decry unfairness to consider how they look at it from only one side of a ledger. Maybe Jesus wanted those who decry unfairness to consider how the unfairness could in fact work a blessing or how, in the big picture, it's not worthy of a complaint. Maybe Jesus wanted us all to realize that God is there for us, not in the giving of unfairness but in our reacting to it. So the next time you say, "It's not fair," take time to give it a second thought.

"I Murdered My Grandmother This Morning!"

Scripture Lesson: Mark 7:31-37

At once, the man's ears were opened.

The failure to listen can be hazardous to our health.

The story goes that Franklin Delano Roosevelt got tired of smiling that big smile and saying the usual things at all those White House receptions. So, one evening, he decided to find out whether anyone was paying attention to what he was saying. As each person came up to him with an extended hand, he flashed that big smile and said: "I murdered my grandmother this morning." Most of the responses went as follows: "Wonderful!" "That's great!" "Glad to hear it!" "Keep up the good work!" Roosevelt found rather quickly that few, if any, were listening to what he had to say.

Now, unfortunately, what Roosevelt encountered at that White House reception is not all that unusual. Not too many of us are good at listening. We may hear but we don't listen. Subsequently, a lot happens that shouldn't have to happen; a lot goes on that shouldn't have to go on. If more of us truly listened, the quality of life would improve not only for ourselves but also for those around us and for the community in which we live.

First of all you'd have better mental health. Sam Kamelson of World Vision International tells of a seventy-year-old lady in Melbourne, Australia, who went to her minister to inquire as to what she might do to help serve the Lord. Unsure how to advise her, he suggested that she go home and pray over it. She did that and the Lord seemed to give her a plan. She bought a batch of three by five cards and wrote on them: "Would you like someone to talk to? Come to my house for tea at 4 p.m." She listed her name at the bottom. Next she posted those little cards around the University of Melbourne.

For the next two weeks this little lady had tea ready at four every afternoon but nobody came. Then, on the following Monday, one Indonesian student arrived and had tea and he found in her someone whom he felt truly listened to what he had to say. When word hit the campus as to what a good listener she was, her teas were filled with students and, when she died several years later, hundreds came to her funeral eternally grateful for the help she had given them at those listening sessions.

Now, that woman had no training in psychology. She had no training in counseling. The only gift she had was that of a good listener, but what a wonderful gift it proved to be. Many on that Melbourne campus had been experiencing immense amounts of tension and turmoil and distress. What they needed was someone to listen to their grief. She fulfilled that need!

One psychiatrist said recently that if everyone really learned to listen to other people, 75 percent of the psychotherapists in the United States would be out of work by next Tuesday. So if more of us truly listened, the mental health of the community would improve immensely. And so would be the case for physical health.

There's a great German tale about Death being struck down and wounded by a giant. As he lay there helplessly, a young man came by who bandaged his wounds and cleaned him up and gave him a drink. After being helped to his feet, Death said to the young man: "Don't you recognize me?" "No, I don't," said the young man. "Well, I am Death and I spare no one. When someone encounters me, he must come with me. I make no exceptions. However, in order to show my appreciation for what you did, I will not take you with me now and, when I do have to call your name, I'll send messengers to give you a fair warning."

The young man was pleased that he would live safe from the fear of death, so he went out and lived a happy and carefree life. As he advanced toward old age, he began experiencing various ailments but he thought nothing of them because he knew he was safe from death. No messenger had as yet arrived. All of a sudden, one day, he turned and he saw Death standing beside him, and Death said: "Follow me! Your hour of departure from the world has come!" "Wait a minute!" said the man. "You promised to send messengers before you arrived and no one's been here!" "I'm surprised that you haven't recognized my messengers," said Death. "I sent fever to slow you down. Next, arthritis came attacking your joints warning you that any step may be your last. Later, infection came and gave you aches and pains all over your body. Finally, I sent fatigue and sleep to remind you each night that Death was near." The man had nothing to say. He yielded to his fate and walked away with Death.

The fable in many ways is true to life. Quite often our body sends out messages letting us know that we're pushing too hard, letting us know that our burning the candle at both ends is exacting its toll, telling us that our dishonesty, our game-playing, isn't boding well with the organs inside us. High blood pressure, headaches, stomachaches, and fatigue are just a few of the ways our body speaks to us. Unfortunately, all too often, we don't listen and as a result our bodies break down a lot sooner than they need to or should.

If more of us began to listen, we'd find better mental health in our community, better physical health, and we'd also find better personal health. Dr. John A. Hutton, who was for many years the editor of *The British Weekly*, told about the dictatorial manner of the caddies who work the golf links at St. Andrew's in Scotland. The caddies, most of whom have worked there for years, usually hand the golfer the proper club, tell him the direction toward which he is to swing, and then watch the performance in silence.

On one occasion a stranger, who was not familiar with the dictatorial manner of the caddies, was preparing to tee off on one of those dogleg holes where the pin is hidden from view and one has to approach the green in an indirect way. In this particular instance, the caddie hands him a golf club and says: "Shoot toward that roofed shed over on your left!" "Wouldn't it be better," said the stranger, "to go straight toward the hole over the trees?" "You may play in any direction you like!" the caddie noted. "I was only suggesting the correct way to do it."

In life today, there are many caddies around telling us the correct way to hit the ball and they are far less dictatorial than those at St. Andrew's in Scotland. They are our grandparents, our parents, our spouse, our friends, our teachers, our ancestors. Their expertise, however, isn't in golf, it's in life. They're telling us things we need to hear. They're telling us what worked in the past when certain difficulties had arisen. They're telling us about opportunities that are out here for the taking, opportunities that will enhance and enrich a life. They're telling us about certain changes we need to make in our lifestyle, changes that will spare us heavy pain. They're telling us about things we're doing that we need to stop doing. There are all kinds of caddies out there in life whose advice, whose counsel, whose wisdom, whose warning are readily being offered, readily and constantly being articulated. But unfortunately, we're not listening, we're not paying attention, and as a result we're hitting bad shots and we're playing poorly. We're talking here not about golf but about life.

If more of us began to listen, we'd find better mental health, better physical health, better personal health, and better civic health.

On the eve of the French Revolution, Louis XVI presided at the opening of the States General in France. The Bishop of Nancy delivered an address in which he described the appalling conditions of the country. He told of the poverty. He told of those who were starving. He told of the beatings that went on. He told of the diseases that were prevalent. He told of the horrible injustices that had been inflicted on so much of the population. While telling of those horrible things, he looked toward the King and there he was fast asleep, his snores growing more audible by the minute. Because Louis XVI didn't listen, the country of France met with disaster.

Although there are many good things going on in this land we live in, there are many who are not doing so well, many who are barely making ends meet, many who are living in poverty, who wander the streets homeless and abandoned. There are also a lot of injustices that still go on and a lot of inequality that has yet to be rectified. But unfortunately, when they're brought to our attention, we don't listen. We may not be as crude as Louis XVI and actually fill the air with snores, but we basically have the news go through one ear and out the other. And because we do so, because so many of us fail to listen to the cries of those who are hurting, the quality of life in this land we live in remains seriously infected. Who knows what disasters may lie in the future.

If more of us began to listen, we'd find better mental health, better personal health, better physical health, better civic health, and finally we'd find better spiritual health.

A colleague of mine said that he once stopped at a street corner where the Salvation Army had gathered. They were soliciting money for Christmas and were filling the air with music. A lovely young woman stood in the circle singing a solo. Around her was the band: the drums, trombone, and cymbals. From the occasional notes he caught of the singer, he judged that the girl had an exceptional voice. He wanted to hear more of it but the blare of the trumpet and the pounding of the drums smothered the solo and drowned out her voice.

That often happens when it comes to the voice of God. God may be speaking but we're not hearing God because we're doing all the talking. We're trumpeting out all our needs. We're drumming up a storm recounting which areas of our life need God's attention. In so doing, we drown out God's voice. If in our prayer life we spoke less and listened more, God might get heard and we just might find our spiritual lives improving quite dramatically.

In our Gospel today, Jesus opens up the ears of someone who was deaf, and in no time he could hear. Our hope and prayer today is that Jesus might open up our ears, not so much that we might hear, because we can, but more importantly and most especially to open our ears that we might listen. That we might listen, first of all, to the many people around us who are hurting and who can't find anyone hosting an afternoon tea that will hear out their hurts. We want Jesus to open up our ears that we might listen to our bodies so when they send out messages, we'll pay attention.

We want Jesus to open our ears that we might listen to the caddies of life when they offer their counsel, their wisdom, and their advice; that we might listen instead of snore when reports emerge telling us of the plight of those who aren't as privileged as we. We want Jesus to open our ears that we might listen when God speaks and get out of the habit of drowning him out with the hammering of our drums and the blasting of our trumpets. If Jesus does that for us, the mental health, the physical health, the personal health, the civic health, and the spiritual health of our community will never be better.

At that White House reception I was referring to earlier, there was one person who did listen to what the President said. It happened to be a foreign diplomat who was looking for some aid for his country. When Roosevelt shook his hand and said he murdered his grandmother, he replied: "Mr. President, sir, she must have had it coming!"

A Word Of Thanks

Scripture Lesson: Luke 17:11-19
"Was there no one to return and give thanks to God?"

Dr. Ernest Campbell, one of the great preachers of our day, called Thanksgiving the most difficult feast on which to preach because, once you've stated the obvious, there's little left to say. Here's an effort to provide a "little left to say."

Rudyard Kipling was one of those authors who was very successful in his lifetime. A British newspaper criticized him and ridiculed him and called him a mercenary. They said: "He is now writing just for the money. One word of Rudyard Kipling is worth $100." Shortly after the release of the unkind article, a reporter approached Kipling at a gathering and said: "So you are worth $100 a word, here is $100, give me a word." Then he handed him a paper and pencil. Kipling took the $100, put it in his pocket, and on the paper he wrote one word, "Thanks," and he gave it to the reporter.

I begin with that anecdote from the life of Rudyard Kipling because I would like to talk with you about the word "thanks" and in particular its lack of application to a whole host of things that often escape our attention. We are quick to use the word "thanks" for favors that are bestowed, gifts that are received, and kindnesses that are granted. But we are not so quick to use it at other times where the blessings received are either far from obvious or under the guise of something that hardly resembles a blessing. Bear with me as I note people, places, and things that we never give much thought to when it comes to the delivery of a word of "thanks."

First there are those responsible for the items and objects that are at arm's length each and every day. Martin Luther King, Jr., liked to remind people that, before they came to a Sunday morning worship service, they touched base with more than half the globe. "When you get up in the morning," he said, "you reached for a bar of soap whose ingredients came by way of France. You reach for a sponge and that comes your way compliments of someone from Turkey. You reach over for a towel and that comes to your hand thanks to the diligent labor of a Pacific Islander. You go down to the kitchen for a cup of coffee and those coffee beans come compliments of a South American. Then, if you decide on a little bread and jam, it is conceivable that they came to the table from a far and distant land." Martin Luther King, Jr., would thus tell his congregation that in less than an hour after waking, there were people and places from all over the world whose products made their way into their bathrooms and kitchens and, if for some reason they happen to be missing, it would not have been a very good morning. You could thus say today that for starters we might consider delivering a word of "thanks" for those people and places whose products enable us to carry out our morning rituals in uninterrupted fashion.

Then, of course, you have the people who have shaped us and molded us and who are, in essence, responsible for who we are and what we are and how we think. I remember someone once asking how many people there were on Robinson Crusoe's island. If you recall the story, the answer was obvious: one. Robinson Crusoe was all alone on the island. That someone then took issue with that answer pointing out that Crusoe took with him to the island everybody who had taught him anything, everybody whom he imitated or emulated when it came to the living of his life. When Robinson Crusoe stepped foot on that uninhabited island, one could say that his relatives and friends and teachers and guides and mentors were all at his side. They were not with him physically but they were the ones who filled his mind, who provided him with his thoughts and hopes and dreams. You could thus honestly say that a lot of people lived on the island with Robinson Crusoe.

When it comes to the delivery of a word of "thanks," we might not just consider those people and places behind the products and items that compose our morning rituals. We might consider as well all the people who made an impression upon us, all of our relatives and friends who have filled our minds with wonderful thoughts and interests and hopes and dreams which we would not have embraced had their lives not touched ours.

To take this a step further, what about those countless others on the other side of this dimension of life? In the book titled *Everybody's Calvary*,[1] Dr. Allen Walker tells of a young priest who went out to say Mass one day only to see one person in the pew. He thought of having him wait till the next Mass when more would be in attendance but he decided against it and proceeded on. When he got to a line in the Preface, the line which reads, "and now with Angels and Archangels and the whole Company of Heaven, we proclaim your glory and join in their unending hymn of praise!" the young priest stopped dead in his tracks and it dawned on him at that moment that it wasn't just he and the person in the pew at the Mass, there were countless others there as well.

I am reminded of the story of the old priest who was heading home one day after Mass and someone shouted to him in a derisive tone: "Were there many at Mass this morning, Father?" The old priest piped back: "There were millions there: the Angels, the Saints, and the multitudes of Heaven!"

Every time we come together in church we are reminded of this other dimension of life; we're reminded of a land that exists far beyond this one. Who's to say that we haven't been beneficiaries of the grace and goodness of those living in that other dimension of life? Who's to say that there aren't people whom we might know or not know praying for us and, because of those prayers, we've received blessings from someone in that company of heaven, someone living in that land beyond this one? So, perhaps, third on the list as recipients of a word of "thanks" might be one or more of those millions that the old priest mentioned, and along with that one or more, the person whose prayers gained their attention.

Then you have as the recipient of our gratitude that which bears little resemblance to a blessing. I read earlier this year of a young man mentioned only by the name Tommy. He was talking to the Reverend John Powell, a professor at Loyola University in Chicago. Tommy was only 24 years of age and suffering from cancer of the lung. He was just told by his physician that he has only a matter of a few weeks to live. Powell asked him what it was like to be 24 and dying. He answered by saying: "It could be worse!" A shocked Powell said: "It could be worse? Like what?" Tommy's response was: "Well, like being fifty and having no values or ideals, like being fifty and thinking that booze, seducing women, and making money are the real biggies of life."

Tommy's remarkable reply gave me cause to think how, even in the worst of circumstances, one can find something to be thankful for. I'm reminded of what Matthew Henry, the old biblical scholar, once wrote in his journal. He had just been mugged and robbed of his wallet. This is what he wrote: "Lord, I'm thankful, first because I was never robbed before, second I'm thankful that although they took my wallet they did not take my life, and third I'm thankful it was I who was robbed not I who was robbing."

Matthew Henry and Tommy have both illustrated how, if life delivers a stinging blow, there can be something in that sea of pain and misery and outrage which can elicit a word of "thanks." And then there are times when the stinging blow itself elicits a word of "thanks" for what it happens to bring to our attention.

A story is told of an African princess who lived in the heart of the jungle. For years this chieftain's daughter had been told by everyone that she was the most beautiful woman of the entire tribe. Although she had no mirror to view herself, she was convinced that she was a woman of unparalleled beauty. One day an exploring party traveled through that part of Africa. They gave the princess a mirror as a gift. For the first time in her life she was able to see her own reflection. Her immediate reaction was to smash the mirror on the nearest rock. For the first time in her life she knew the truth about her lack of beauty and the truth proved too difficult to handle.

The stinging blows of life often serve as a mirror, getting us to see things we did not want to see, to admit things we did not want to admit, and to face things we did not wish to face. Like that princess, we're not at all happy about receiving such a revelation. We may even be embarrassed or disconsolate over what it brings to our attention. A truth, however, is realized and that warrants a word of "thanks."

Then how about those common, everyday events and occurrences which would never occur to us as subjects of our gratitude. The Jesuit William O'Malley, in one of his books,[2] made some

100

interesting points. He said that it's funny how as kids we were grateful to the tooth fairy for what that person puts under our pillow. Yet we never think of giving thanks for teeth, old and new. As kids, he said, we are grateful to Santa Claus for putting toys in our Christmas stocking, yet we never give thanks for the legs we put in our socks each morning. We ask God for peace in the Middle East and Bosnia and Northern Ireland yet we never thank God for the peace we have had in the United States since 1865. And, in closing, O'Malley asked to consider whether we ever give thanks to God that the sun came up seven times this past week, because it didn't have to, and whether we ever give thanks that we saw the sun rise in the morning because there are tens of thousands who, on one of those seven days, met with death and will never see another sunrise. I could go on with other examples, but you get the idea. There is much that should elicit a word of "thanks" that we entirely take for granted.

Lastly, there are the people who look to us for help. I remember hearing of a minister who had very little money. He was just getting by. One day a destitute family came to him and he was moved to pity. He gave them all the money he had and food as well and as they left he said: "Thank you for the privilege of letting me help you!" The minister sincerely meant what he said for he saw his helping others as an opportunity to be like God, and for that, how could one be anything but thankful? Those who get us to open our wallets, to open our hearts, and to donate our talents should not be the ones giving a word of "thanks." It should be us. We've been provided with the privilege of being like God.

Today's Gospel is the familiar story of the ten lepers who were cured of their disease. Only one provided any show of gratitude. Jesus tells the story to remind us of the importance and necessity of giving thanks. So as we consider the many obvious things for which we need to give God a word of "thanks," it behooves us to think as well of the not-so-obvious things that also deserve a word of "thanks."

We might think of the people from around the world who supply the invaluable products of our morning rituals. We might think of friends and family who have filled our minds with thoughts and hopes and dreams. We might think of a few of those millions from the other dimension of life who have extended to us more than a few blessings. We might think of the stinging blows of life which in themselves or of themselves have given cause for thanks. We might think of sunrises and teeth and legs and a host of other assorted things we take for granted. And we might think as well of those who got us to act like God.

My friends, heed the Gospel! Give God and give others a hearty word of "thanks."

---

1. Alan Walker, *Everybody's Calvary* (London: Epworth Press, 1944).

2. William J. O'Malley S.J., *Why Not* (New York: Alba House, 1986).

It's All The Same To Me

Scripture Lesson: Acts 10:25-26, 34-35, 44-48
   ... Peter entered the house of Cornelius ...

An examination of the types of prejudice of which we're often guilty.

A Chinese and a Jewish individual were eating lunch together when, without warning, the Jewish man got up and slapped the Chinese gentleman across the face. The Chinese gent was stunned! Rubbing his jaw, he said: "What in the world did you do that for?" And the answer came back: "Pearl Harbor." "I didn't have anything to do with Pearl Harbor. It was the Japanese who bombed Pearl Harbor." The Jewish man replied: "Chinese, Japanese, Taiwanese — they're all the same to me."

They each returned to eating their lunch and before long the Chinese gent walks over to the Jewish man and slaps him across the face. The Jewish man yelled out: "What did you do that for?" And the answer came back: "The *Titanic*." "The *Titanic*! I didn't have anything to do with the Titanic. An iceberg brought it down." Whereupon the Chinese man replied: "Iceberg, Goldberg, Ginsberg — they're all the same to me."

I begin with that bit of humor because I'd like to talk with you today about prejudice and I see the joke as revelatory of a mindset responsible for prejudice. Many people, I'm afraid, are much like the two men I just described. They wouldn't hit anybody because of race or nationality or religion, but they do have on their mind this notion that one representative of a race or nation or religion is typical of every representative of a race or nation or religion. The bad of one person becomes the bad of every person; what's true of one is true of all. Although we may claim that we're above reaching similar conclusions, we're not above applying a similar logic. Our prejudice may not involve a race or nationality or religion but

103

it does involve the bad of one person and what we'll do is put that person's entire life under the umbrella of the bad.

Consider the story of Fred Snodgrass, star baseball player for the 1912 New York Giants. In the seventh and deciding game of the World Series that year, he missed a pop fly. His error allowed the winning run to score, costing the Giants the World Series. In 1974 Fred Snodgrass died. *The New York Times* headline read: "Fred Snodgrass, 85, Died — Baseball Player Muffed Fly in 1912." What was remembered about him at the end of his life was the error that cost his team the World Series. After leaving baseball, Fred Snodgrass became a successful rancher and banker. He was so respected in his community that they asked him to run for mayor, a position he was elected to and held for many years. He was a wonderful father who had a beautiful family yet, sadly, what was remembered about him was his mistake.

How often has it happened that a friend or acquaintance makes a mistake or commits a sin and all we ever think about, from that day forward, is that mistake or that sin. The person may repent, may repair the damage of that one sin or that one mistake, and may go and do an unbelievable number of wonderful things. All of that, however, gets left out of the equation when we see that person. We'll always hold a prejudice for that one sin or that one mistake.

There are people, for example, who have filed bankruptcy, who are recovering alcoholics, who have left the priesthood or the religious life, who committed a crime, who are HIV positive, and unfortunately they'll forever be victims of prejudice because people will always mention them in regards to their bankruptcy, their alcoholism, their crime, or their former state in life.

Then you have as a provider of prejudice, the mindset that takes everything at face value, that sees something and automatically registers a subsequent and final opinion. I'm reminded of the time when Nikita Khrushchev came to the United States and, at the start of one of his speeches, clasped his hands above his head and jumped up and down. Americans were furious. Not long beforehand, he boasted that Russia will bury us and here he was jumping up and down like a cocky prizefighter who had just triumphed in a boxing match.

104

Some years later a man familiar with the culture was asked about that incident. He related the fact that the gestures of Khrushchev were not those of a cocky prizefighter. Those gestures, he said, were a Russian sign of friendship and of peace. In Russia, clasping hands above one's head and jumping up and down are meant to symbolize hands clasped in friendship across the sea.

It makes us stop and think of times we've jumped to conclusions about people based on something unique to their culture. Many a prejudice stems from our misinterpretation of some habit or gesture that means something totally opposite of what it appears to be. Along similar lines, there is the mindset where the misinterpretation doesn't involve something unique to a culture or race but does involve something that isn't what it seems.

Gessen was a Buddhist monk who was an exceptionally talented artist. Before he would start painting, he required payment in advance and what he normally charged was exorbitant. He became known as the greedy monk. Typical among his customers was a fairly wealthy woman who, upon paying him, said to someone: "This man is supposed to be a monk, but all he thinks about is money. His talent is exceptional but he has a filthy money-loving mind."

Many years later, quite by chance, someone found out why Gessen was so eager for money. It was discovered that he came from a part of the province where famine was a regular part of life. His heart ached for its victims so he built barns and filled them with grain and when a famine struck he made arrangements for the grain to be taken to families that were hurting. This was all done in secret. The families did not know from whence came the grain. Gessen was also "eager for money" because the main road leading to the city was in such bad condition that ox carts would constantly tip and fall. This presented untold hardships for the aged and the infirm who needed to get to the city for the health care it provided. Gessen had the road repaired. The final reason he was "eager for money" was so that he might build a meditation temple which his teacher wanted desperately for the province but could never secure the funds. When all those important needs were secured, Gessen stopped painting and went back to being a Buddhist monk.

How often have we drawn conclusions about people based on outward activity, based on what they're doing, having not a clue as to what might happen to lie behind their behavior. Many a prejudice is a product of a mind that fails to ask questions, that fails to make inquiries, that automatically passes judgment without ever considering the possibility that there's something causing the victim of their prejudice to behave in the way they're behaving.

Another provider of prejudice is the mindset that denies the existence of any truth other than its own. I'm reminded here of that scene from *Alice in Wonderland* where there's a trial just beginning and the king calls for the rabbit to read the accusation that prompted the trial. After the accusation is read, the king quickly turns to the jury and inquires as to their verdict. At that point, the horrified rabbit jumps to its feet and says: "Not yet, your majesty! There's a great deal that needs to happen before that."

There are many people today who are like that king — quick to rush to a verdict before evidence is heard. They are the people who would say: "I've made up my mind. Don't confuse me with the facts!"

When Galileo was summoned to court for the heresy of claiming the earth revolved around the sun, he brought his telescope with him and set it up in the courtroom. When the judge read the charge against him, Galileo invited the judge and the others on the inquisition panel to look through the telescope. He had set it so that they could see the Moons of Jupiter, something that would prove him right. The judge and the inquisition panel refused to look through the telescope. They were convinced that the Earth did not revolve around the sun and no evidence would convince them otherwise.

Too many of us have a prejudice when it comes to proponents of new theories, new ideas, new ways of looking at things. Like that judge and that inquisition panel, we dismiss all of them without giving them so much as a hearing. We're convinced that there can't possibly be any truth other than the ones we happen to hold.

Then there's the prejudice born in a previous generation. I'm reminded of a song from the popular play *South Pacific*. It's sung by a nurse who happens to be a victim of racial prejudice. She tells in the song how children are taught to hate, how they're born color blind and unprejudiced only to be tainted by adults who put into their heads animosities and resentments they couldn't possibly attain on their own. Many a prejudice stems from something of long ago that should have been forgotten but gets passed down from one generation to the next.

An incident took place several years ago involving the Serbian leader Slobodan Milosevic. He's standing on a patch of ground telling a huge crowd of young Serbs how on the very ground on which they're standing a massacre took place. The Bosnians brutalized a thousand Serbs. He told the story with vengeance in his eyes and hatred in his heart. It so riled the young crowd that they left that patch of ground with animosity toward every Bosnian. The brutalization, the massacre to which he referred, took place in the thirteenth century. Many a prejudice is a product of an old incident that's unfortunately been kept alive for far too many years and has gotten passed on to far too many generations.

I've been talking about prejudice today because we find Peter in our first reading taking a huge step in dismantling a prejudice that he and most Jews had held for many generations. Peter, all of his life, had never called on a Gentile. He was to stay away from them for they were unclean. So he had been taught. So he had been told. When he called on Cornelius, he crossed a racial barrier and he found, to his astonishment, a friend on the other side. He says to Cornelius: "And to me God hath shone that I should never call any man common or unclean."

We are called today to take a long and deep look at our practice of prejudice so we might dismantle ours as Peter dismantled his. That means we need look beyond people's sins or mistakes. We need to recognize that Fred Snodgrass may have dropped a fly ball but that was one blemish on an otherwise beautiful and successful life. We need, as well, to do some reading, some research, some exploring so we won't stupidly pass judgment, so we won't call a monk like Gessen greedy or a Russian like Khrushchev cocky when the facts say otherwise. If we hope to dismantle our prejudice as Peter dismantled his, we need to keep from providing a verdict without looking at the evidence; we need at least to look through the telescope. We need not to let history dictate our vision. We need to return to the mind of our infant days, a mind that was colorless and unprejudiced, a mind where "Chinese, Japanese, Taiwanese, Iceberg, Ginsberg, Goldberg are not the same to me."

How Thinking

Scripture Lesson: Luke 16:1-13
"... take your invoice, sit down quickly, and make it fifty ..."

A troublesome parable that seems to praise dishonesty. We need to look at the mindset and not the practice of the manager as the reason for his positive mention.

———————

The sales manager of a highly successful company was asked about his method for training salespeople especially when it comes to the obstacles and difficulties prevalent in the world of business. He said that he makes it a point to stress the importance of their being a "how" thinker in deference to an "if" thinker. The "if" thinker, he explained, will brood over a difficulty or setback and bitterly say: "If I had only done this or if I had only done that!" A "how" thinker, on the other hand, will look at that same difficulty or setback and eagerly say: "How can I do better the next time? How can I use this to my advantage?" The sales manager went on to say that if those under his charge think in terms of "how" and not in terms of "if," record sales will be registered.

That sales manager, I believe, was on to something that works wonders not only in the world of business but also works wonders in the world of life. Great things happen, extraordinary accomplishments are had, wonderful events occur, welcome changes and innovations come to pass thanks to "how" thinkers, thanks to those who, when obstacles and difficulties arise, think of how some good can be accomplished despite the many barriers standing in the way.

A study was done of 300 highly successful people, people such as Winston Churchill, Helen Keller, Ghandi, Martin Luther King, Jr., to name a few. It was found that one quarter had such handicaps as blindness, deafness, crippled limbs. Three-quarters had either been born into poverty or came from broken homes. The overwhelming majority entered into life under the worst of conditions and circumstances. They could have easily said: "If only I didn't have those burdens and difficulties placed upon me, if only I could have been born differently." Instead, however, they made the best of a bad situation. They were "how" thinkers and not "if" thinkers and, as such, they found a way to overcome the burdens and difficulties and obstacles which could have easily kept them from achieving the greatness they achieved.

I read an interesting anecdote concerning Gene Tunney, who became the heavyweight boxing champion of the world when he defeated Jack Dempsey many years ago. Tunney began his career as a hard puncher and many of his victories came by way of a knockout. When he went on a tour of exhibition bouts as a member of the American Armed Forces in World War I, he broke his hand. The doctor and his manager told him he would never be able to punch as he once had because the break revealed a condition that would forever leave him with brittle hands. It seemed that Tunney's dream of being heavyweight champion of the world would never be realized. Tunney, however, was not dismayed. He said: "If I can't become the champion as a puncher, I will make it as a boxer." So Tunney went to work as a student of the art of self-defense. He would soon become one of the most scientific and skillful boxers ever to step into the squared circle. His newfound skills as a boxer enabled him to outbox and defeat Jack Dempsey for the heavyweight championship of the world.

Examining that feat, experts claim that Tunney would never have been able to win that title as a puncher. It was the art of self-defense, it was the scientific skills of boxing that provided him with the victory. Tunney could have looked at his brittle hands and figured all was lost. He would have thus spent the rest of his life with a lot of "if onlys" running through his mind. But Tunney, being a "how" thinker, found a way to still accomplish his dream despite a condition that appeared to doom it.

Whether a person is born with a problem or disadvantage or falls victim to one along life's way, the difference maker, that which turns drudgery into victory, that which turns tragedy into a means for greatness, rests on whether one thinks in terms of "if" or whether one thinks in terms of "how." It is the "how" thinker who realizes the victory and the greatness.

And it is the "how" thinkers, as well, who are a breath of fresh air. A sheepherder in Indiana was troubled by his neighbors' dogs that were killing his sheep. The normal and usual way to counter the problem was by lawsuits, barbed wire fences, or even shotguns. This particular herder saw a need for a better idea. So what he did was give every neighbors' child a lamb or two as pets and, in due time, when all his neighbors had their own small flocks of sheep, they realized they had to keep their dogs tied up. They did so each and every day.

The sheepherder could have easily resorted to the old solution to the problem. He could have thought in terms of "if": "If I got enough barbed wire, if I shot a few of their dogs, if I file a few law suits!" That would have only resulted in animosity and tension between himself and his neighbors. But the sheepherder, being a "how" thinker, thought how he might resolve the problem without jeopardizing his relationships with his neighbors.

"How" thinkers are a breath of fresh air because, instead of dealing with the problems in a way they have been dealt with for years, they carve a different path. That path provides a welcome change to what had previously been the usual order of business.

I am reminded of a father whose son was killed at the hand of the Japanese. He was, as you might well imagine, filled with deep grief and with deep anger toward the Japanese. After the funeral, however, he did something that astonished everyone. He made a huge donation to the International Christian University in Tokyo, Japan. When asked why he would do such a thing, the father explained that he believed that the Japanese boy who killed his son was probably no different than his own boy and that his boy, in similar circumstances with the roles reversed, most likely would have acted in much the same way. By donating money to a Christian University in Japan, he hoped that programs could be developed whereby Japanese children could learn the ways and means of conducting life without warfare, of settling differences without the necessity of taking a human life.

Now, that father was a "how" thinker par excellence. He could have easily resorted to the usual order of business and lived his days in bitterness and anger toward the Japanese for what they did to his son, but he carved a different path. He thought in terms of how he might help put an end to what he surmised as being the real cause of his son's tragedy, and that was war. That father's donation to the Christian University was a breath of fresh air, a welcome change from the thirst for vengeance and retaliation that usually follows a tragedy such as his.

"How" thinkers provide a breath of fresh air, "how" thinkers accomplish greatness despite obstacles and hardships, and "how" thinkers also make things happen.

One of the favorite stories of Salvation Army Founder General William Booth concerned a little girl who worried herself sick because birds kept getting caught in traps set by her older brother John. "O Lord," she prayed, "don't let the little birds get caught in John's traps! Please don't let them!" And then, to her mother's astonishment, she added exultantly: "Oh, I know they won't, they can't! Amen!" Her mother quickly admonished her daughter, asking how she could be so sure that God was going to answer her prayer for the little birds. The daughter replied: "Well, Mom, before I prayed, I went out onto the yard and I smashed all the traps!"

The funny story brings home another aspect of "how" thinkers. That is the realization that you can't sit back and expect things to happen, you can't just wish and pray and hope that what you wish and pray for will come true. The "how" thinker is always considering how the best might come to pass, how the best might be furthered along, how their prayers (a la the little girl) might be guaranteed a positive answer. In contrast to wondering *if* good things are going to happen, the "how" thinkers are calculating *how* good things are going to happen.

"How" thinkers provide a breath of fresh air, "how" thinkers accomplish greatness despite obstacles and hardships, "how" thinkers make things happen and, lastly, "how" thinkers are always one step ahead of everyone else.

The owner of a successful drill company decided to retire. He put his son in charge of the operation. Two days later, this son called a meeting and asked the four vice presidents what they saw the company doing over the next five years. Pretty much in unison, they spoke of looking at new shapes and sizes for the drills and of finding new and different ways of marketing them across the country. Before another word was said, the new owner of the company dropped a bombshell. "Friends, I have news for you," he said. "We are no longer going to sell drills." The four vice presidents couldn't believe the announcement and in unison they cried: "If we are not going to sell drills, what are we going to sell?" The new owner announced: "From now on, we are going to sell holes! People don't want to buy drills, they want to buy what drills do for them, they want to buy holes!" And, with that, the company began an exploration of new ways of making holes, eventually coming upon the development of lasers which could, with a beam of light, cut a hole faster and better than any drill.

The innovators, the trail blazers, the pioneers, those who are on the cutting edge of life and industry, those outdistancing all the competition, are of a similar ilk to the new owner of that drill factory. They are "how" thinkers. While those in the "if" mold are wondering if they can stay competitive, these creative individuals are in the "how" mold wondering how they might move into the future, how they might find new and better and more ingenious ways of doing things. "How" thinkers have the vision to see an abundance of possibilities and opportunities in places and in situations where the "if" thinker is standing still.

I have reviewed with you all of the positives of "how" thinkers because as I read today's Gospel parable, Jesus gives such thinkers high praise. The parable has been a problem for many of us because it has Jesus seemingly condoning dishonest behavior. It has Jesus acclaiming a manager who, by changing those invoices, was cheating his boss. What we need to understand is that Jesus is not condoning the dishonesty or the cheating, he's merely recognizing the positive fact that the manager did not sit and bewail and grow bitter over the loss of his job. Instead, he immediately came upon a way to make the best of a bad situation. In essence, the manager could have said or cried: "If only this didn't happen to me!" Instead, he said: "How can I pick myself up and start anew?" The manager was a "how" thinker and not an "if" thinker.

Jesus, in telling today's parable, was looking for his hearers to be like that manager, to think in "how" terms. That would mean not letting brittle hands keep us from realizing our dreams. That would mean finding ways to use our defects and our deficiencies and hardships to our advantage. That would mean that we provide the world with a breath of fresh air by not choosing to do what has always been done when we have been hurt or slighted or when dogs are killing our sheep. That would mean our smashing the traps before we pray, our doing what we can to make things happen. That would mean our thinking beyond drills to holes, our having a vision to see beyond today.

My friends, be a "how" thinker and not an "if" thinker! Not only will you excel in life but you'll win God's praise. You'll be reflecting God's glory.

The Power Of Little Things

Scripture Lesson: Mark 4:26-34
*"... It is like mustard seed ... the smallest of all the earth's seeds
... yet ... springs up to become the largest of shrubs ..."*

A mustard seed yields power in different ways.

We are all, I believe, familiar with the story of the *Titanic*. An unsinkable ship on its maiden voyage strikes an iceberg. The ship goes down, over a thousand people die. It's an amazing story, which is why it's been told not only on the silver screen and on Broadway, but in countless books as well.

I mention the *Titanic* because I'd like to talk with you about the power of little things. It was something little that proved responsible for the sinking of that mighty ship. Back in 1993, Robert Ballard was able to locate the ship's remains. When his underwater cameras circled the ship, they didn't find a huge gash in the hull (which everyone surmised to be the cause of the disaster), but found instead that the rivets from the bow to the middle of the ship were all damaged. Since the survivors of the *Titanic* never felt the ship hit anything, it's believed now that by brushing into an iceberg the rivets began to pop in ripple-like fashion, causing water to enter the ship in different places at once, rendering useless the system designed to make it unsinkable. In essence, what brought down the *Titanic* were rivets no bigger than the head of a large screwdriver.

I'm reminded of an observation Harry Emerson Fosdick made upon encountering some redwood trees in California that met with death. Those redwoods, looking more like skyscrapers than trees, survived hurricanes, tornadoes, earthquakes, and lightning storms over the course of 1,500 years of existence. What caused their deaths was the deterioration of their core thanks to the appetite of tiny beetles no bigger than ants.

The space vehicle *Mariner I*, destined for Mars, suddenly veered off course and into oblivion. A single hyphen was inadvertently left out of the data fed into its guidance system and that was the cause of its regrettable fate.

The people of Rochester several years back had to boil their water for 33 days because of contamination. After a long search, the source of the contamination was discovered to be the fecal material of tiny caterpillars.

Rivets, a tiny beetle, a hyphen, the fecal material of a caterpillar are all samples of the power of little things. The biggest ship ever built, the biggest, strongest trees ever grown, a billion dollar spacecraft, millions of citizens in the Rochester community — they all felt the power and they all give testimony to the negative things that can happen thanks to that power.

It can thus be said that there's more than just a little truth to the old blacksmith creed: "For lack of a nail, the shoe was lost. For lack of a shoe, the horse was lost. For lack of a horse, the general was lost. For lack of a general, the victory was lost. For lack of a victory, the nation was lost."

Now, lest you all despair that the power and the strength and significance of little things only rest in the negative, the great news, the wonderful news, is that it also rests in the positive. Just as a rivet or a hyphen or a beetle can cause monumental harm, so can similar little things cause monumental good.

Think, if you will, of a little boy who wanted to help a group of doctors working in the Third World. He buys a bottle of aspirin, puts it in a package, and he sends it to the Air Force asking if by chance they might drop it by parachute when they fly over that area in the Third World. One of the news wires gets wind of the story and features it on the evening news. Moved by the story, the viewers open up their wallets and before long half a million dollars worth of medical equipment gets shipped to those doctors working in the Third World.

Think, if you will, of Helen Caldicott, an Australian pediatrician, who expressed concern about radiation elements in the milk being fed to children. Her letter to a local newspaper generates a television interview which prompted an investigation which linked the radiation elements to nuclear testing conducted by the French in the Pacific Ocean, testing which France refused to stop. Soon Helen Caldicott found herself as one of a delegation of three who went before the International Court of Justice to complain. The end result was the country of France being forced to stop the testing, something everyone claimed could never be done. In the case of Helen Caldicott and in the case of that young boy, one letter, one bottle of aspirin, was all it took to accomplish monumental good. It had a ripple effect. It became a catalyst mobilizing all kinds of people to work towards a goal that proved to be a benefit to hundreds of thousands of people. Little things can yield positive power by being the start of something good. And little things can yield positive power as well by being the end of something good.

I read recently of the work of stone cutters. When it comes to cutting a huge stone, a stone cutter starts with a big hammer and he whacks the stone. The first time he hits it there's not a chip, a scratch, nothing. He pulls back the hammer and he hits it again. He hits it 100 times, 200 times, 300 times and still not even a scratch. He'll take a breather and come back the next day and do the same thing. People sometimes pass by and laugh at him for persisting when obviously his actions are having no effect. He keeps hitting it over and over and then, on the seven hundredth hit or maybe the one thousandth hit, one single hit will literally break the stone in half.

Positive things of a monumental nature are often one contribution away from becoming a reality. Sometimes it takes only one more letter, only one more word of encouragement, one more vote of confidence, one more small sacrifice, one more tiny good deed and that contribution acts like the one thousandth hit that broke the stone. One small thing we might do in the face of a huge problem might not be the catalyst that mobilizes the numbers necessary to make an impact on the problem, but it could instead be the one which proves to make a critical difference when it comes to that problem's solution.

I read something recently that speaks to the point. I read that when water is heated to 211 degrees Fahrenheit it's simply boiling water. But when the temperature reaches 212 degrees, only one degree higher, the water becomes steam, steam that is powerful enough to launch a Navy jet 120 miles an hour in five seconds from an aircraft carrier. A little thing often yields positive power by being that one degree or that one thousandth hit which proves to make all the difference in the world when it comes to accomplishing what no one thought could ever be accomplished.

Besides what it can do at the end or even the beginning of something good, little things can also exhibit power in the middle of something good. By that I mean a constancy when it comes to the little things that are done.

At Glasgow University, the famous Lord Kelvin used to illustrate the effects of small forces on large masses. In his classroom, he would have a 200-pound lump of steel suspended from the ceiling. He would have a basket of little paper balls and, to the great joy of his class, he would begin to bombard the heavy lump of steel with the tiny paper balls. At first nothing happened but, in time, the lump of steel would tremble and then it would begin to move and then it would literally swing back and forth, all thanks to the repeated blows of little paper balls. Little things can achieve big things if we keep doing them. It's the keeping at it that gets big things to move.

I'm reminded here of Hope Haremould who heard of a prisoner in Indonesia who was unjustly incarcerated. She learned the man's name from Amnesty International. Government officials and people with considerable influence spoke on the prisoner's behalf but to no avail. The old woman decided to take up the cause herself. She started writing one letter after another with impassioned pleas for his release. She wrote to every government official in Indonesia. She wrote the guards who took care of the prisoner. She wrote to everyone imaginable. She kept writing, and writing, and writing. Sometime later she got a letter from the prisoner who was finally set free. What turned the tide was a government rule which stated that all letters in regard to a prisoner had to be kept on file and the flood of letters from the pen of Hope Haremould so thickened the file, that it took up more space than the cabinet could hold. This so overwhelmed prison officials that they felt it better to release the prisoner than deal with all those letters. It could thus be said that Hope Haremould hit the Indonesian government with small paper balls and, by so doing, accomplished what all sorts of powerful groups and powerful government officials weren't able to accomplish.

When Jesus in our Gospel parable spoke in terms of a mustard seed, he was outlining for us the power of little things. He was letting us know that we should never underestimate the power that can be generated from what might appear to be small and insignificant. Like a mustard seed, there's no telling as to the magnitude of its possibilities.

My friends, if you look around, you'll see problems of such immensity that you'll figure there's nothing you can do which will really matter. If you look around, you'll find yourself up against a lot of what may appear as impossible to do anything about. The fact is, however, that you never know the power that's contained in some small thing that you're capable of doing.

Your one letter of protest might, like Helen Caldicott, result in the halting of an activity everyone thought was impossible to stop. Your letter, your voice of concern, your act of generosity, your doing something small might actually be the one thousandth hit of a stone or the one degree increase in temperature that makes all the difference in the world. And don't forget! If you consistently keep doing what seems small and not likely to matter, just remember the experiment in that Glasgow laboratory, just remember Hope Haremould. You might get an immovable situation to sway in a positive direction. My friends, be the rivet, be the beetle, be the hyphen, but be it in a positive way. Keep planting your mustard seed; you never know the heights to which it can reach.

Feeling Tired

Scripture Lesson: Matthew 11:25-30
"Come to me, all you who are weary ..."

A reflection on what may be the source of our tiredness.

During the last 24 hours each of our hearts has beat 104,000 times, our blood has traveled 168,000 miles, we breathed 24,000 breaths, and we have inhaled 438 cubic feet of air. We perspired a pint of fluid, we exercised 7,000 brain cells, and we moved 750 muscles. We spoke 4,800 words and generated 450 tons of energy. If you wonder why you are feeling tired, that's the reason. And to make matters worse, you have to do it all over again tomorrow.

All of what I have told you is true as far as the facts are concerned, but as far as citing that as the reason for our tiredness, that's not true. Our tiredness is a result of many things. It is those many things that I would like to talk with you about today. With the numbers of us feeling tired and exhausted, with so many of us yearning for rest, I thought it timely to review what could well be the sources and the reasons for our tiredness.

First of all, it could be that we are overly consumed by the work ethic. While on vacation, a successful businessman visited an Indian village. As he walked along, he saw a man lying under a tree doing nothing. This prompted him to say: "Hey, Chief, don't you think it time to be up and about doing something productive?" The man under the tree looked up and replied: "Why?" The businessman answered: "So you can get a job, earn some money, and make something of yourself." The man under the tree simply smiled and again said: "Why?" Very annoyed, the businessman retorted: "So you can make money, start a savings account, and then someday you can retire and enjoy life." The man under the tree simply smiled and said: "I am enjoying life now."

Now I am not trying to throw stones at the work ethic. God knows it's in need of restoration. But many of us, unfortunately, are terrorized by that ethic. Engraved in our heads is this notion that we are nothing unless we are working. Anything resembling enjoyment is anathema. That successful businessman I just mentioned captured the philosophy well. The fatal flaw, of course, is our lack of enjoyment of the present moment and the failure to take time "to smell the roses." We thus distance ourselves from the very thing that can invigorate us, energize us, and relax us.

The second reason for our tiredness and exhaustion may be the kind of work that we happen to be doing. In the wonderful musical comedy *Showboat*, one of the lead characters, Captain Andy, periodically sings out a bit of philosophy. In one of the scenes, he sings that "the lucky folk are the ones who get to do things they enjoy doing." How right he is! Not only are those folk lucky, but they're also very seldom tired. It has been shown time and time again that those who are in a job they like, in a line of work they enjoy, have unbelievable energy and they are tremendously happy. They hardly ever complain of fatigue or tiredness or exhaustion.

Thomas Edison's wife worried that he worked too much and deserved and needed a vacation. Mrs. Edison wasn't about to make a suggestion as to where he should go; that would have to be his decision. But she felt it important that he spend some time away from his work. After months of prodding by his wife, Thomas Edison finally agreed to go on a vacation. His elated wife said to him: "Look! You have enough money! Just decide where you would rather be than anywhere else on earth and go there." "Very well," he replied. "I will go tomorrow." The next day he faithfully kept his promise. He went back to his laboratory. It happened to be the place he'd rather be than any place else in the world.

People whom Captain Andy described as being lucky, people who enjoy their work, seldom get tired and fatigued no matter how many hours they spend at work. If we are feeling tired and exhausted, it could well be that we are in a line of work we do not like. And if not that, maybe it's simply a case of being bored.

I heard a mother describe a scene not atypical of young people today. She was telling that her daughter comes home from work totally exhausted with barely enough energy to eat her meal. Afterwards, she struggles desperately to keep from falling asleep.

Suddenly the phone rings and a friend offers the possibility of going out to a nightspot. In seconds, the girl springs to life. In no time, she's changing clothes and in minutes she's out the door and off to "do the town." She'll party until 2 or 3 in the morning showing no sign of fatigue or exhaustion. For many, tiredness is more a product of boredom than a product of physical exertion.

If it isn't boredom that's at fault, monotony might well be the reason for our tiredness. John Moffat, the noted translator of the New Testament, used to have three tables in his study. One contained the manuscript of his translation of the New Testament that, for him, was an ongoing work. On another table, there sat a manuscript of a work on Tertullian on which he was also engaged. On the third table was a manuscript of a detective novel that he also happened to be working on. What Moffat did for rest was to move from one table to another. As his "battery" got drained, he'd "jump start" it by moving to another table where he'd find a manuscript which engaged different skills, interests, and talents. For many people, tiredness and exhaustion come from a limited set of interests, from the failure to possess more than one means to occupy one's attention.

If it isn't monotony or boredom, it could be the matter of negative emotions sapping one's stamina, strength, and animation. Hans Selye, famed for his work on stress, told of a painful incident in his life which he had kept inside him for many years. It occurred in medical school and it involved the theft of his research findings by a supposed friend. He came to the conclusion that he could either let go of that hurt or he could continue to let it fester inside him. He chose the former and, as a means of letting go of the hurt, he wrote his memoirs, getting onto paper what was sitting deep inside him. That action amounted to the lifting of a sixteen-ton weight from his shoulders. The subsequent exhilaration provided him with new life. He was no longer as tired and exhausted as he once had been.

That is one of the problems with bitterness and anger and resentment and thoughts of vengeance and retribution. They weigh us down, they take their toll on our power, our energy, and our strength. It could well be that the source for our tiredness and exhaustion is that we have not been able to let go of some hurt deep inside us, that we have not been able to practice the art of forgiveness, either of which might have done for us what the writing of those memoirs did for Hans Selye.

There is the possibility that the source of our tiredness stems from the lack of a cause greater than ourselves. Ellen Langer, a leading social psychologist, ran an experiment in a nursing home. A particular group of residents were given a number of houseplants that they were to water and care for and supervise. Langer discovered that their involvement in that simple task increased their alertness, added to their energy, and provided them with enthusiasm for life.

I am reminded of a story of a group of women who worked eight to ten hours a day in a parachute factory crouching over sewing machines and stitching endless lengths of colorless fabric. It was a taxing and exhausting job. When World War II began, they were told that their job was critical to the war effort. The lives of their sons and grandsons and husbands could very well be riding on what they happened to be stitching and sewing. Learning the news, they not only worked much more enthusiastically but they also showed little evidence of tiredness and exhaustion.

When people are involved in a cause greater than they are, when they give of themselves for someone or something other than themselves, there comes with it a surge of energy, a feeling of exhilaration and a feeling of positive accomplishment, and that can do wonders for the relief of tiredness and exhaustion and fatigue.

Finally, as a cause for the lack of stamina and energy and vitality, there's the matter of frustration. In 1891, Lord Randolph Churchill, the father of Sir Winston Churchill, wrote to his wife that in all probability more than two-thirds of his life was over and he did not want to spend any more time beating his head against a stone wall. Lord Randolph Churchill was a leader in the British government and a champion of many important causes, but he was finding his work and efforts only receiving abuse and apathy. He was growing tired and exhausted and planned to resign his position the next day.

Unfortunately, what Lord Randolph was experiencing comes with the territory for those involved in the work of social justice.

Those who stand for what's right, those who speak for the poor and powerless often get beaten down and worn down and exhausted. What they need is to look at those who were biblical giants when it came to social justice, people like Moses or Isaiah or Jeremiah or Jesus. What kept them from exhaustion and despair and tiredness was the fact that they knew that what they were doing was right and just and of God.

The Gospel today has that famed and oft quoted line of Jesus: "Come to me all you who labor and are heavy burdened and I will give you rest. Take my yoke upon your shoulder and learn from me for I am meek and humble of heart. Your soul will find rest and my yoke is easy and my burden light." Jesus is telling us who are tired and exhausted to look to him for rest. Looking to him might mean putting a lid on our work ethic and taking the time to smell the roses. It might mean being exhorted to begin looking for a job we'll like. It could be that we who are exhausted and tired because of boredom or monotony or the lack of a cause bigger than ourselves might have to put into our lives a diversity of activity that will engage not only our curiosity and our interest but will also be of help to the community.

Looking to Jesus for rest might mean his pushing us to let go and forgive, his pushing us to snap away the chains of bitterness and resentment. And for those of us who are exhausted and tired because we seem to be getting nowhere in our work for social justice, looking to Jesus for rest could find him connecting us to the "batteries" of Moses and Isaiah and Jeremiah. To all who are tired and exhausted, Jesus says: "Come to me and I will give you rest."

Rejection

Scripture Lesson: Matthew 21:33-43
"... the stone which the builders rejected ..."

Some balm for the wound of rejection.

———————————

When I was in high school, if there was someone we didn't like, if there was someone who ticked us off, if there was someone we didn't want to be associated with, we'd call that someone a "reject." Compared to the X-rated name-calling in vogue in high schools of today, that's pretty mild. But when you think about it, the term "reject" did pack a wallop. If there's one thing a teenager fears and loathes, it's rejection. And that goes not just for teenagers; it goes for adults and young children as well.

Generally speaking, we can handle physical punishment. Our minds can endure stress. Our hearts can absorb a loss. But we're not very good at handling or enduring or absorbing rejection. It has power to wipe smiles off our faces, to buckle our knees, to stoop our shoulders, and even to break our hearts. As a result, we'll do everything possible to resist and avoid it.

There are people who buy clothes they don't like. There are people who drink and do not like it. There are people who applaud things they detest, who agree with something that's against their principles, all because they fear the rejection that may follow should they fail to do so.

I could talk with you today about how wrong that is, but what I'd like to talk with you about is the feeling of rejection. No matter how hard we try to resist and avoid it, it's inevitable that we experience rejection. Bear with me as I try to list some things to consider should rejection come our way.

First and foremost, perhaps the rejection was brought on by ourselves. Many years ago in France, those who were employed in the various factories of that country occasionally encountered excessive abuse at the hands of the owners of those factories. When that occurred, their means of retaliation involved the hurling of their wooden shoes into the guts of the machines which they operated. This would cause the machines to jam, thus bringing the factory to a standstill. The wooden shoes were called *sabots*. The word sabotage was derived from it.

All too often we sabotage a relationship, we sabotage a job opportunity, and we sabotage ourselves by throwing into our minds the wooden shoes of negativism and defeatism virtually guaranteeing our rejection. I know of people who have gone to a job interview not only looking shabby but also so down and so negative that the employer would be crazy to hire them. I know of people who bemoan their lack of friends while at the same time displaying a self-centeredness and a cynicism that would repel a Mother Teresa. I know of people who automatically assume rejection, never bothering to check whether their assumptions were true. Many times we are victims of rejection that we brought on ourselves. We need to assume responsibility for the rejection and embark on a change in attitude, a change in temperament, or just a reversal of the negative, defeatist thinking that can make acceptance impossible.

The second thing to consider when we experience rejection is that maybe it couldn't be helped. I refer here to those who reject us but who never intended rejection but because of fear or awkwardness or misunderstanding, it turned out that way.

One of the most difficult things experienced by parents of a stillborn baby is their rejection by some of their friends, especially those who are expectant parents. Many times it's because those friends fear that stillbirths might be contagious; many times those friends don't know what to say or do so, as a result, they keep their distance. It's wrong but it happens.

A similar case can be made for cancer patients or any victims of a tragedy. The people you thought you could count on the most for support and strength are often nowhere to be found. A good deal of the time it stems from fear, from awkwardness, from ignorance, or from not wanting to face the grief of seeing you hurting. I hate to say that it can't be helped, but human nature being what it is, many times people don't really intend rejection but it turns out that way.

128

The third thing to consider when we experience rejection is that maybe we've got it all wrong, maybe we haven't been rejected at all. A man and a woman were driving from Minneapolis to Ft. Lauderdale to begin a three-day second honeymoon celebrating their 25th wedding anniversary. As they moved along at the 55-mile per hour speed limit, they came upon a beat-up old clunker barely cruising at 40 miles per hour. Two young people were inside, a boy and a girl, close together, obviously much in love. "Walter," said Eleanor, "why don't we ever sit together like that anymore?" Walter kept his eyes straight on the road, his hands firmly on the wheel, and quietly said: "Well, I haven't moved!"

We can smile at that, but it's a good description of the rejection we might feel when it comes to God, even when it comes to our friends. We might feel rejection and believe it from the nature of what we've done or what we're experiencing, but it's often us that's done the moving away, not them.

The fourth thing to consider when we experience rejection is that maybe it's for our own good. I was reading recently about what is considered to be one of the most amazing births to witness, the birth of a giraffe. First of all the mother gives birth to the baby standing up so the newborn falls ten feet to the hard ground when it leaves the womb. What adds insult to injury is what comes next. The mother giraffe lowers her head long enough to take a quick look and then positions herself directly over her calf. She waits for a minute or two and she then swings her leg and kicks her baby, sending the calf sprawling head over heels. She'll keep doing it over and over until the calf stands up. And then, once the calf is standing, the mother will knock it off its feet one more time.

Those who happen to be observing the birth process are horrified. How could the mother giraffe be so cruel? But zoologists will tell you that every mother giraffe will do that to its newborn because kicking them that way teaches them to stand up. Their kicking them again once they're standing is a way to get the calf to remember it. In a jungle where baby giraffes are open prey to lions and tigers and all sorts of natural enemies, that's crucial to their survival because if a calf can't stand and walk in a hurry it will soon be somebody's meal.

Sometimes rejection can be similar to that kicking. Loved ones might reject loved ones because they feel that's the only way to get the person they love to wake up to the fact that they have a problem and that they must deal with that problem. It's the only way to get a loved one to stop hurting oneself and one's family. It's called tough love and many times rejection is a part of tough love.

The fifth thing to consider when we experience rejection is that it might be a badge of honor. Anthony de Mello, the late Jesuit mystic, tells of a social worker who poured out her woes to the Zen Master. She told him how much good she would be able to do for the poor if she did not have to spend so much time and energy defending herself and her work from a barrage of criticism. The Zen Master listened attentively and then responded in a single sentence. He said to her: "No one throws stones at barren trees!" That's a good piece of advice for many who because of their morality or their excellence find themselves victims of rejection.

I'm sorry for youth in school who are talented or who excel in their studies. I'm sorry for young men and young women who wish to preserve their virginity for the marriage bed. I'm sorry for kids who refuse to join a gang, who resist the pressure to engage in bad activities. I'm sorry because quite often the end result is their rejection by their peers. But you know what? The Zen Master is right! "No one throws stones at barren trees!" They should raise their heads high and look at their rejection in those situations as a badge of honor.

The sixth thing to consider when we experience rejection is that many talented people and great people have been where we are. A six-year-old boy came home from school with a note saying: "Keep the boy at home! He's backward and unteachable!" The boy's name was Albert Einstein. Wallace Johnson worked in a sawmill, a valued and honored employee, he thought, till he got the infamous pink rejection slip. He went on to become the founder of the Holiday Inn hotel chain. The famous sculptor Rodin was rejected three straight times when he applied to art school. After Fred Astaire's first screen test, he was rejected. The testing director wrote: "Can't act! Slightly bald! Can dance a little!" And get this: Ronald Reagan was rejected for a leading role in a 1969 movie because he didn't look presidential. Just because you've been rejected, it's not the end of the world. Many great and famous people have been there and have gone on to do great things.

That brings me at long last to the basis for this sermon. Jesus, himself no stranger to rejection, tells in today's Gospel parable about how God provided for his people only to meet with rejection. Then, the famous line is uttered: "The stone, which the builders rejected, has become the cornerstone." So we have in Jesus, we have in God, someone who knew full well the feeling and experience of rejection but never allowed the rejection to affect the building of the kingdom, making it, in fact, its very cornerstone. Most especially and most beautifully, they never allowed the rejection to stop them from loving us.

I'm reminded of that *Chicken Soup for the Soul* story of Chad who one day came home from school and told his mother that he'd like to make a valentine for everyone in his class. Her heart sank because she knew how Chad had been shut out by his classmates. She noticed that when he came home from school his classmates laughed and hung on to each other and talked to each other but Chad was never included. He walked behind them by himself. She feared, therefore, that he'd give everyone a valentine and not receive a single one in return. Nevertheless, she went along with Chad and for three weeks helped him to make personal valentines for each of his 35 classmates.

Valentine's Day came. Chad was beside himself in excitement. He carefully stacked up the valentines and put them in a bag and bolted out the door. Poor Mom was worried sick all day fearing the feeling of rejection Chad might experience if he didn't get any cards in return. While watching for him to come home from school, her heart sank because there was Chad tailing behind his classmates and carrying no valentines. As he came to the door, she stood there ready to embrace him. He stopped in the doorway to say: "Not a one! Not a one!" And then with a big smile and a glow to his face, he said: "Not a one! I didn't forget a single one with my valentines, not a one!"

Jesus and God are like Chad. Although rejected by many, they still love. That love misses not a one, not a single one!

My friends, if you feel rejected consider the possibility that maybe you brought it on yourself, maybe it couldn't be helped, maybe you've got it all wrong, maybe the rejection was for your own good, maybe it's a badge of honor, or maybe like those famous people it will be a catalyst for greater things.

But most of all and most especially, if you're feeling rejection, God still loves you. God hasn't moved from the steering wheel. God identifies with your rejection. And even if you don't think you deserve God's love, it's there because God's love doesn't miss a one, not a single one!

Seven Deadly Virtues

Scripture Lesson: 1 Corinthians 12:31—13:13
If I have faith great enough to move mountains,
but have not love, I'm nothing.

We are all familiar with the seven deadly sins. Here is a look at a few virtues that can, at times, be deadly!

When we first entered St. John Vianney Seminary in East Aurora in 1969, my classmates and I found the political atmosphere not to our liking. As had been our experience, we were expecting to have some input into the policies and procedures of that institution, but we came to realize that its mode of governance did not allow for that. Any form of democracy was simply not allowed. We knew that you can't have the inmates running the asylum, but we thought that our views and ideas should at least be heard and that the seminary would be better served if students were an integral part of their decision-making process.

Whether we wore them down or they came around to our way of thinking, we gradually over the years began to have some input into polices and procedures. Much to our delight and elation, democracy began to emerge in the governance of the seminary.

A year and a half before I was to graduate, an interesting turn of events took place. Christ the King Seminary in Olean relocated itself at our St. John Vianney Campus, literally taking over the campus lock, stock, and barrel. Although we found it quite unsettling, we were at least comforted by the fact that the new administration espoused a democratic form of governance not unlike what we had worked so hard to establish with the outgoing administration. Much to our horror and consternation and disbelief, however, we found that majority rule and student input quickly resulted in the rolling back of freedoms we had won and the restoration of things we had fought to eliminate. We came to realize that our way of thinking was not the way of thinking of the seminarians who transferred to our campus. They now constituted the majority.

The democratic form of governance, which we regarded as a virtue, became for us a vice. What we held up as a blessing became for us a curse. What we considered a positive became for us a negative. A good thing became for us a bad thing.

I begin with that interesting experience in my seminary life because I'd like to talk with you today about good things becoming bad things. I'd like to talk with you about things that deserve our acclaim becoming things that deserve our disdain. You've heard about the seven deadly sins. Well, I'd like to present to you what could be called the seven deadly virtues.

I begin with patience, a virtue whose positive credentials can't be denied. If Thomas Edison hadn't had patience, he would never have been able to overcome the multiple failures that preceded most of his inventions. If it weren't for patience, Anne Sullivan would never have been able to continue her teaching lessons and the world would have been denied the likes of a Helen Keller. People described as having the patience of Job are people held in high esteem.

But as positive and as acclaimed as is the virtue of patience, there are times when patience is anything but virtuous. I liked that cartoon that shows a man in his fifties dressed in a baseball hat and baseball suit, clutching a baseball bat. He's seated on an easy chair with a telephone at his side. Across from him sits his wife with frustration written all over her face. The caption reads: "I don't want to step on your dream, Walter! But if they haven't called you in over thirty years perhaps it's time to move on to something else."

Sometimes patience is a cover for stubbornness, sometimes it's a cover for laziness, and sometimes it's an excuse designed to avoid a change or a move that needs to be made. How often have we seen social activists calling attention to an injustice or crime only to have us counsel them for patience just so we wouldn't have to bother with or get involved with the resolution of that crime or injustice.

Second on the list of deadly virtues is honesty. With all the deceit that's rampant in Washington and with the growing proliferation of "rip-off" artists, and with phoniness encountered in so

many places, we all yearn for honesty. We all yearn ⸝⸜
ing. But, once again, like patience, there are times and o⸜⸜
when honesty and truth telling can be less than virtuous.

We've all heard the long-running joke about the patient who
went to see his doctor. The doctor says: "The trouble with you is
that you're too fat!" The patient, in anger, barks back: "I demand a
second opinion!" "Okay!" said the doctor. "You're ugly too!"

Many times, the practice of honesty can take on the crassness
of that doctor. Many brilliant people are honest in their remarks
but that honesty comes out of spite and arrogance as they rip apart
those less gifted than themselves. Many prejudiced people are honest in their remarks but the honesty is laced with venom as they
openly castigate a race of people they do not like. Many who are
mean-spirited have a reputation for honesty but the honesty is exercised to degrade and diminish anyone who stands in their way.
Honesty can indeed, at times, be less than virtuous.

A third deadly virtue is kindness. In these times when more
and more people appear rude and callous, we long for the practice
of kindness and we delight in its display. But, then again, like patience and honesty, there are times where kindness is anything but
virtuous.

You might remember the old story of the little boy who adopted
a turtle for a pet. One day the turtle rolled over on its back and died.
The boy was heartbroken and could not be consoled. His mother
called his dad who rushed home from work to help the boy in his
grief. After a few failed attempts at consolation, the father said:
"Look, Son, here's what we'll do. We'll have a little funeral ceremony. You can invite your friends. We'll put the turtle in my silver
cigarette box and we'll process to the backyard. You can lead the
way with a candle and once there we'll bury him next to the rose-
bush. Afterwards, we'll get some ice cream and cookies and have a
party." By this time, the boy's tears came to a halt. He was now
smiling from ear to ear. It was precisely at that moment when the
turtle everyone thought was dead flipped over on its legs and walked
away. The boy looked to his dad and said: "Let's kill it!"

Many times we do kind things, we do nice things, strictly for
our benefit. We use it as an avenue for favors or we see it for its

pay back potential. Many an act of kindness thus comes not out of the generosity of our hearts but out of the selfishness of our souls. The turtle, who was seemingly the beneficiary of our kindness, might well be someone we neither care about nor like. Kindness can indeed at times be less than virtuous.

The fourth deadly virtue is compassion. Like kindness, it too is sorely needed in this cold and callous world in which we live. But also, like kindness, there are times when compassion is anything but virtuous.

A woman in Washington was pulled over by the police and handed a $200 ticket because she and her three passengers were not wearing their seat belts. She pleaded for compassion and mercy on the part of the officer but to no avail. Two days later, she was involved in a horrible accident and because she and her passengers had their seat belts fastened they were saved from mortal injury. She admitted after the accident that, had that police officer shown compassion and not given her that expensive ticket, she wouldn't have been as vigilant in securing her seat belt as well as those of her passengers.

Compassion can sometimes be the reason addicts stay addicted and careless people stay careless and irresponsible people stay irresponsible. People often need to face their problems and assume responsibility. For them, compassion (as evidenced by that driver and her passengers) could well perpetuate what needs to stop. Compassion can indeed, at times, be less than virtuous.

Fifth on the list of deadly virtues is piety. I don't believe many will argue with the need to be more reverent or the need to be more prayerful. God bless those pious people whose prayers have gotten more than a few of us through difficult times. But like patience and kindness and compassion and honesty, there are times where piety is anything but virtuous.

Several women were visiting an elderly friend who had taken ill. When they rose to leave, they told her: "We'll keep you in our prayers." The ailing woman says to them: "Look, why don't you go in the kitchen and wash the dishes and clean the floor? I can do my own praying!"

Piety can often be a convenient escape from involving oneself in the needs and difficulties of another person. It can often, as well, be a facade providing a lazy and mean and self-centered person with a camouflage for his laziness or meanness or self-centeredness. Piety can indeed, at times, be less than virtuous.

The sixth deadly virtue is righteousness. *Boston Globe* columnist Linda Weltner tells of sitting in a park watching children at play. Two children get into an argument and one says to the other: "I hate you! I'm never going to play with you again!" For a few minutes they play separately and then they're back as friends, sharing their toys just as they did before.

Ms. Weltner remarks to another mother: "How do children do that? How do they manage to be so angry with each other one minute and the best of friends the next?" The other mother answers: "It's easy! They choose happiness over righteousness!"

Righteousness is indeed virtuous, but when it gets chosen over forgiveness, when it gets chosen over justice, when it gets chosen over happiness, when it's an excuse for our arrogance and stubbornness, we're looking at something that's less than virtuous.

In the seventh and final spot on the list of deadly virtues is loyalty. We appreciate loyalty, we praise loyalty, and we may even have gone so far as to say that it's heroic to be loyal! But like patience and compassion and kindness and righteousness and piety and honesty, there are times when loyalty is anything but virtuous.

All I need do is point to the loyalty of the followers of Jim Jones or the followers of David Koresh; all I need do is point to those who refuse to look at the facts, who refuse to hear the truth of a new revelation. You can see how loyalty can become deadly, how loyalty can be less than virtuous.

Our second reading today has been hailed as the most beautiful in all of Sacred Scripture. It's been called the great hymn of love. You find within it a great list of virtues: speaking with angelic tongues, being prophetic, having faith to move mountains, giving our bodies to be burned for a good cause, feeding the poor. These are wonderful and noble virtues and actions. But note what Paul says! He says they are all good for nothing if they're not animated with love.

So it goes with the virtues of patience and honesty and kindness and compassion and piety and righteousness and loyalty and I'll toss in democracy. If there isn't a love for God running through it, if there isn't a love for justice, if there isn't a love for truth, if love is absent from any virtue, they are no more than a "noisy gong or a clanging bell"; they are anything but virtuous.

So, my friends, be people of virtue! But be sure the virtue doesn't turn deadly.

the meeting in the first place. It then dawned on him that he didn't have to, that what he really needed was not the solution to a special problem but an association with a special person. He needed to be in the presence of someone who exuded confidence and nobility and high energy. He needed to be with someone whose excitement about life proved contagious, who transmitted a spirit that captivated his soul.

One of the main causes of burnout is a run on one's batteries by people who fail to share the same idealism, who fail to share the same outlook on life. Those very same people usually hammer home the point that what we're doing is a waste of time. They usually pepper us with both criticism and cynicism. If we hope to keep burnout at bay, we desperately need to seek out and enjoy the company of people of the ilk of a Phillips Brooks, people who exude a spirit similar to our own, people who provide a much needed charge to a battery drained by the cynic, the doubter, and the defeatist who so often command our attention.

Lastly in that wine cellar, Jesus placed a bottle that has God's name written all over it. A young sailor was told during a terrific storm to climb the mast and trim the sails. As he got halfway up the mast, he made the mistake of looking down. The roll of the ship combined with the tossing of the waves made for a gasp of fright. The young man started to lose his balance and was about to fall when an older sailor started to shout: "Look up, Son, look up!" The young sailor did so and regained his balance. To keep ourselves from falling into burnout and discouragement, it's important that we hold our heads high, that we keep our heads pointed in the direction of God, for it's God who is our refuge and our strength, a stronghold that gives us safety, an anchor for keeping our spirits high.

My friends, there are indeed a lot of people in life similar to that pioneer of BAMM whom I interviewed several years back. They're burned out. They've run out of wine. The good news is that, just as Jesus helped those in Cana, he can help us. He's furnished a cellar filled with his wine.

There's the red heifer wine letting us know we're an imperfect people in an imperfect world. There's the mud wine letting us know that the mud we're mired in is the stuff of rubies and emeralds and diamonds. There's the future-based wine letting us know that although we might not enjoy the fruits of our labor, there will be someone who will. There's the wine with a Phillips Brooks label letting us know our need to hang with high-spirited people. There's the wine with a God label reminding us to look to God when the sea of life gets rough and discouragement is near.

Jesus has provided us with a wine cellar so that in the event that we seem to be running out of wine, there's a place to go where your supply may be replenished. My friends, if you're burned out or close to it, find that wine cellar. It might be what the doctor ordered to recover your spirit or to maintain the flame burning ever so small inside you.

Who's To Say?

Scripture Lesson: Isaiah 45:1, 4-6

... Cyrus, whose right hand I grasp ...

When something good occurs as two people meet, it could well have been orchestrated by God.

I think it is safe to say that all of us are creatures of habit. We tend to go through various daily routines and rituals and seldom do we ever break from those routines or rituals. So when something possesses us to do so, it tends to be memorable.

One morning, not long ago, heading over to the hospital from my room at the School of Nursing, I had such a memorable experience. I stopped by the switchboard, as I usually do, to check whether the computer printouts had been picked up. If they haven't, I'll take them to the office and, if they have, I'll proceed to the cafeteria. That's my habit, that's my routine.

That particular morning, the papers were picked up. As I took a few steps towards the cafeteria I stopped and, for some strange reason, did something I usually don't do. I turned around and headed for the office. I was going to do something I usually do after breakfast. As I waited for the elevator, someone came hurriedly around the corner. It was the wife of a patient I had gotten to know in ICU. As soon as she saw me, she started to cry, telling me that the hospital had just called to say her husband had taken a turn for the worse. I embraced her and we walked arm-in-arm all the way to ICU. When we got there, her husband had improved. He was holding his own. Considerably relieved, the wife proceeded to thank me profusely for being there. When she got to the hospital, she had no idea how she was going to make it to ICU. The fact that I was there when she got to the elevator made all the difference in the world.

Now, what possessed me to break from my usual morning routine, something that I seldom, if ever, do? What possessed me to be at that elevator just at the time she arrived at the hospital? I think that the answer can be found in our first reading today.

Cyrus, the Persian king, happened to arrive on the world scene just when God's people needed him the most. Isaiah sees his timely arrival as the hand of God at work in the world. Cyrus wasn't aware of that. He wasn't even a believer. Yet Isaiah tells us that even though he knew it not, God used him to do some good in the world.

I couldn't help but think that what happened to Cyrus happened to me on that particular morning at Sisters Hospital. Even though I didn't know it at the time, even though I had no inkling of God invading my life, who's to say that that wasn't precisely what happened? Though I knew it not, God used me to work some good in the world.

I cannot but recall that piece from Charles Dickens' *A Tale of Two Cities*[1] where two people are being taken to the guillotine. One of them is a young man who took the place of his friend. The other is a young girl, terribly frightened. When she sees the strength and the calmness in the young man's face, she says to him: "Give me your hand that I may have some of your strength." He gave her his hand and as they arrived at the guillotine, she said to him: "Thank you. I think you were sent to me by God."

Now, we're talking fiction here, of course, but who's to say that at times we're not sent by God to places where our presence, our interaction, our words provide something that positively influences the life of someone else? Like Cyrus, we wouldn't be aware of that, we wouldn't realize that. But who is to say that God doesn't use us? Who's to say that God doesn't arrange for us to be in the presence of people in need, of people who are hurting, of people who are on the brink of making a terrible decision? Who's to say that, unbeknownst to them and us, God decided to be of help and used our words, our presence, and our interaction with them to provide that help?

Besides our being used by God or being sent by God, who's to say, as well, that we haven't been on the receiving end of such an action? Who's to say that God hasn't used someone to affect us, to uplift us, or to move us into an action or activity that has brightened the dark world in which we happen to live?

That could well be the case with the young nun who for twenty years taught the wealthiest children in the land where she happened to work. One night walking down the street she heard a woman call for help. Realizing the seriousness of her condition, she rushed her to the hospital where she was told to sit and wait. She knew the woman would die without immediate attention so she took her to another hospital. Again she was told to wait. The woman's social caste made her less important than the others being treated. Finally, in desperation, she took the woman home, and later that night she died in her arms. That encounter would change that nun's life. She decided to quit her teaching and begin establishing clinics and homes devoted to the poor and the dying. She wanted to make sure that they would be treated with the dignity and the respect that they deserve. That nun I'm referring to is Mother Teresa.

Now who is to say that God didn't use that dying woman unbeknownst to her and to Mother Teresa? Who's to say that that dying woman wasn't a vehicle that God ordained so that Mother Teresa could begin the great work that she did?

Think in your own lives how you got involved in Mother Teresa type activities. Think about ways you may have found yourself volunteering for something that required sacrifice and giving on your part. I'll bet that for some of you it was because a special someone touched your life at the right time and in the right place and moved you to volunteer. It could well be that God used that special someone unbeknownst to both of you. It could well be that God played a part in your life as God did in the life of Mother Teresa. I would think the same holds true for countless others engaged in activities bringing light to this darkened world.

Harry Emerson Fosdick says that we can see the hand of God in all the discoveries and all the revelations that came from the scientific laboratories all across the land. Many of the cures and many of the insights into genetics, many of the various breakthroughs for some of the chronic disorders that plague our world came and come our way compliments of people used by God. They may not be religious at all. They may not even be believers. Nonetheless, like Cyrus in our first reading, God didn't hesitate to use their life to bring forth good in the world. So, it could be you or it could be me, it could be a stranger or someone you know, it could be a believer or a non-believer. No one is exempt from being a vehicle of God for God often chooses to use a life unbeknownst to the inhabiter of that life.

Samuel Miller was Dean of the Divinity School at Harvard for many years. He recalled once a pantomime performed on the stage of the Bavarian Opera House. The pantomime began with a stage that was bare except for one circle of light. A clown began to search very diligently for something he had lost. After a time, a policeman came up and asked: "Have you lost something?" "The key to my house," replied the clown. "If I can't find it, I can't go home tonight!" With that, the policeman joined in the search with great intensity. Finally he asked: "Are you sure you lost it here?" "Oh, no, I lost it over there," said the clown, pointing to the darkened part of the stage. "Then why on earth are you looking here?" "Because there is no light over there!"

That humorous pantomime captures a tendency that we all have to look for God where the light happens to be shining. We figure God to use people in the religious or social limelight to dispense his grace. But the truth is that God is more likely to be at work in the shadows, tapping unknown, unsuspecting, and unlikely individuals to be vehicles of his grace in offices and stores and streets, away from the lights of the cameras recording the nightly news.

William Wolcott, a great English artist, came to New York City in 1924 to record his impressions of the skyscraper city. He found himself one morning in the architect's office of a colleague for whom he had worked years before in England. Suddenly, the urge to sketch came over him. He quickly said to his colleague: "Please, I need some paper!" Seeing some paper on the desk, he said: "May I have that?" The architectural colleague said: "That's not sketching paper, Mr. Wolcott, that's just ordinary wrapping paper." Wolcott, not wanting to lose the inspiration, reached out and said: "Nothing is ordinary if you know how to use it!" He took the wrapping paper and made two sketches. One sold for a thousand dollars and the other for five hundred dollars.

Like Wolcott, God doesn't hesitate to use whatever is available to work good in the world. He might use ordinary people like you and me or he might use a Cyrus-type, some Nobel Prize winner or head of state, or he might use an obscure, dying woman in Calcutta. There is no telling whom God might use to sketch for someone the hope, the inspiration, the strength, the insight that will impact either his or her own life, the life of someone else, the life of the world, or all three.

F. W. Robertson is a name few of you would know. He was a famous preacher who worked a lot of good in his role as a minister. For his life's work, he wanted to be a soldier as his father and grandfather had been and as his three brothers were. The problem was that he could not secure a commission, so he ended up taking the advice of a friend and went to Oxford to prepare for the Christian ministry. Five days after his arrival at Oxford, the military commission came. He longed to accept it, but he felt he had pledged himself to be a minister and could not go back on his pledge. Nobody now doubts that ministry was his true calling or that if ever a man was designed for ministry, Robertson was.

In papers found after he died, Robertson reflected on the fact that had he not met that friend who advised him to go to Oxford, he would have probably been a soldier. If he had not known a certain lady, he would not have met that friend. He mused that perhaps that woman and that friend were used by God to move his life in the direction that it took.

Indeed, who's to say that God didn't use me when I met that wife of the patient at the door of that elevator? Who's to say that a friend of yours, an acquaintance of yours, wasn't used by God to get you to perform some loving, charitable action? Who's to say that God won't use us to work some good in someone's life, and who's to say that God won't send someone to us to work some good in our lives? Like Cyrus, it can happen unbeknownst to us. God works the shadows. God sketches with anything he can find. So next time you break from a habit, it might be God using you for one of his inspirations.

---

1. Charles Dickens, *A Tale of Two Cities* (London: J. B. Lippincot Co., 1930).